Risk Management: CIMA CGMA Strategic Level

Azhar ul Haque Sario

Copyright

First Printing, 2025

Azhar.sario@hotmail.co.uk

ORCID: https://orcid.org/0009-0004-8629-830X
LinkedIn: https://www.linkedin.com/in/azharulhaquesario/

Disclaimer: This book is free from AI use. The cover was designed in Canva.

Disclaimer: The author has no affiliation with the Chartered Institute of Management Accountants (CIMA). This book is independently produced under the principle of nominative fair use to help students prepare for their exams.

Contents

Area A: Enterprise Risk

Analyse Sources and Types of Risk

The Unseen Currents: A Guide to the Risks We Navigate

Every venture, every organization, is a ship setting sail on a vast and unpredictable ocean. We have a destination in mind—our goals, our vision for success. But the journey is never a straight line on a calm sea. It's a constant dance with the wind and the waves, with hidden reefs and sudden squalls. This is the world of risk. It's not a line item on a spreadsheet; it's the very water we sail on. Understanding it means learning to be a better captain.

Part 1: The Shifting Seas: Where Do Risks Begin?

Risk isn't born in a vacuum. It whispers from the engine room, brews in the distant clouds, and is charted in the decisions made on the bridge. To master it, we must first know its many faces.

The Hum of the Engine Room (Operational Risks): Down in the heart of our ship, the day-to-day work gets done. Here, a thousand things can go wrong. A piston misfires (equipment failure). A crew member misreads a gauge (human error). A critical shipment of fuel from a port is delayed (supply chain disruption). These aren't grand, dramatic events, but small, internal failures that can slow us down, cause damage, or even leave us dead in the water. They are the constant, grinding friction of doing business.

The Captain's Chart (Strategic Risks): On the bridge, the captain pores over the maps, choosing a course. This is where the big gambles are made. Do we sail for that newly discovered island (a new market)? Do we invest in a radical new type of sail (a new technology)? What if the island is already claimed by a powerful rival? What if the new sail rips in the first strong wind? These are the risks of ambition. A wrong turn here doesn't just get you lost; it can lead you straight into a hurricane or leave you becalmed for years, watching other ships sail over the horizon.

The Ship's Coffers (Financial Risks): A ship needs supplies. It needs fuel. It needs a crew that's paid. The financial health of our vessel is its lifeblood. But the value of currencies can shift like treacherous currents, making our foreign-earned treasure worth less when we get it home. The cost of borrowing money can rise like the tide, threatening to swamp our budgets. A sudden economic drought can dry up the very ports we trade with. Managing the coffers is a constant battle to ensure we don't run out of provisions mid-voyage.

The Unpredictable Weather (External Risks): Some risks have nothing to do with our ship or our crew. They are the fundamental forces of the ocean itself. A massive economic storm (a recession) can churn the waters for everyone. A diplomatic feud between two naval powers (a trade war) can close entire shipping lanes. A technological tsunami—a groundbreaking innovation by someone else—can create a wave that makes our entire vessel obsolete overnight. And in the digital fog, cyber-pirates are constantly probing for a way to board our systems and plunder our data. We cannot control the weather, but we must be prepared to navigate it.

The Law of the Sea (Regulatory & Legal Risks): The oceans aren't lawless. The great maritime powers (governments) create rules. Maps are dotted with "Here be dragons" warnings about environmental zones, data privacy territories, and labor laws. Ignoring these rules can bring the full force of a navy down upon you, with crippling fines and sanctions that can tarnish your flag forever. This isn't just about following the rules; it's about anticipating how the rules will change tomorrow.

Part 2: Naming the Monsters: A Field Guide to Risk

Once we know where to look, we can start naming the beasts that swim in these waters. Giving them a name strips them of their power and helps us forge the right weapons to fight them.

The Kraken of the Bottom Line (Financial Risk): This is the most famous monster, the one that attacks the treasure chest directly. It can take the form of market shifts that devalue your cargo, credit defaults where another captain's promise of payment turns out to be a lie, or a liquidity crisis where you're stranded with no wind (cash) to fill your sails. This beast's only goal is to pull your enterprise into the red depths.

The Gremlins in the Works (Operational Risk): These aren't giant sea monsters; they are small, mischievous creatures that chew on the ropes, misalign the compass, and clog the pumps. They are the risk of your own machinery, people, and processes failing you from the inside out. A single gremlin—a data entry typo, a missed safety check—

can seem harmless, but a swarm of them can sink the sturdiest ship.

The Siren's Call of Yesterday (Strategic Risk): This is perhaps the most seductive danger. It's the beautiful, alluring song that whispers, "Stay here. The way you've always done it is safe." It lures captains toward the rocks of obsolescence while newer, faster ships discover new worlds. It's the risk of clinging to an old, faded map while the very shape of the continents is changing.

The Leviathan of Regulation (Compliance Risk): This colossal beast doesn't care about your intentions. It patrols the seas with an ironclad book of rules. If you cross into its territory—violating a data law, an environmental standard, or a trade statute—its judgment is swift and heavy. Fighting this monster requires not just a lawyer, but a culture of vigilance that runs through the entire crew.

The Phantom Echo (Reputational Risk): In the modern sea, every ship leaves a wake, and every story travels on the wind. This risk is a ghost. A single oil spill, a scandal on the captain's deck, or a rumor of mistreating the crew can create a phantom echo that follows you. Other ports will refuse to trade with you. The best sailors will refuse to serve under your flag. This monster doesn't sink your ship with force; it isolates you until you starve. It attacks your name, which is often your most valuable asset.

The Digital Pirates (Cybersecurity Risk): A new breed of threat for a new age of sailing. These pirates don't swing on ropes; they slide through firewalls. They can steal your maps (intellectual property), hold your navigation systems for ransom, and listen to every secret conversation on board. They can damage your ship from thousands of miles away, proving that in today's world, the most dangerous waters may be the invisible ones.

In the end, risk is not something to be eliminated. A waveless sea is a windless sea, and ships don't move without wind. The goal is to become a master mariner—to build a sturdy vessel, to train a vigilant crew, to read the weather, to understand the monsters, and to navigate with courage and wisdom. The sea is never truly calm, but for those who respect its power, the journey is everything.

Upside and downside risks

The Alchemist's Gamble: Turning Risk into Gold

In the heart of every business, there's a simmering cauldron. It's the cauldron of uncertainty, where every decision, every market shift, and every new idea is an ingredient tossed into the mix. We call this potent brew "risk." But to see risk as just a poison to be avoided is to miss the point entirely. The greatest alchemists of enterprise know the truth: risk is both the deadliest poison and the elixir of life. It's the volatile agent that can either blow up the laboratory or transmute lead into gold. This is the duality of our craft: managing the shadows of downside risk while courageously chasing the light of upside potential.

The Shadows: Taming the Volatile Brew

When we speak of risk, our minds instinctively conjure images of failure—the cracked vial, the toxic plume, the experiment gone horribly wrong. These are the downside risks, the myriad ways our great work can curdle and collapse.

Think of the very foundation of our lab: our finances. The brew is threatened by market risk, where the fires of the market flicker unpredictably, devaluing the precious metals in our coffers. It's haunted by credit risk, the ghost of a partner who promises payment but vanishes, leaving our own accounts empty. A sudden liquidity crisis is the terrifying moment we find ourselves with a vault full of treasure but unable to buy the daily bread needed to keep the apprentices fed—a fatal inability to convert assets to cash.

But the dangers are not just in our ledgers. They are in the very mechanics of our work. These are the operational risks. It could be a simple human error—an alchemist mistaking salt for sugar, a single misplaced ingredient that ruins the entire concoction. It could be a failure of our equipment—the astrolabe that guides our timing suddenly cracks, or our central furnace (the server) goes cold, bringing the entire process to a standstill. Or perhaps the caravan carrying the rare herbs we need from a distant land is lost to a storm, a stark reminder of our fragile supply chains.

Looming over it all are the grand, existential threats—the strategic risks. What if a rival alchemist discovers a faster, cheaper way to make gold, making our life's work obsolete overnight? That is the terror of technological obsolescence. What if the King, once our greatest patron, is swayed by rumors that our work is heresy? That is reputational risk, a poison that can taint our name for generations, no matter how pure our intentions.

Managing these shadows isn't about trying to create a world with no risk. That would be like trying to practice alchemy without fire. It's impossible and sterile. Instead, it's about being a master of the craft. It's about building a sturdier laboratory, knowing the precise boiling point of every ingredient, and having the neutralizing potion ready the moment the brew begins to bubble over.

The Light: Distilling Pure Opportunity

Now, let us speak of the magic. Let us speak of the upside. If we focus only on preventing explosions, we will never create anything of value. The true genius of alchemy lies in embracing the same volatile elements that threaten us and using their power to create something magnificent. Upside risks are the whispers of possibility, the unexpected reactions that, if harnessed, can lead to breakthroughs beyond our wildest dreams.

The most potent source of upside is innovation. Imagine, while attempting to create a simple healing tonic, you accidentally stumble upon the formula for a revolutionary new source of energy. This is the magic of research and development. It's about having the courage to mix ingredients that have never been mixed before, knowing that while most attempts will fizzle, one might just illuminate the world. Embracing emerging sciences, like artificial intelligence, is like discovering a new elemental language—it can unlock secrets and efficiencies we never thought possible.

Sometimes, the world itself presents a gift. A sudden shift in the zeitgeist, a newfound public craving for the very thing you specialize in—this is the upside of market expansion. It's like discovering that a common garden weed in your possession is, in fact, a rare and coveted spice in a neighboring kingdom. Are you ready to harvest it? Can you scale your garden quickly enough to meet the demand?

And what of our fellow alchemists? A strategic partnership can be the most powerful catalyst of all. By combining your knowledge of rare metals with another's mastery of ancient texts, you might create something that neither of you could ever have created alone. This synergy is the essence of collaborative upside, turning two promising workshops into a legendary guild.

Even the King's decree, so often a source of fear, can be an unexpected boon. A new law banning the use of mercury in alchemy might seem like a crippling regulatory blow. But for you, the only alchemist who has already perfected a mercury-free process, it's a golden ticket. The new rule has just eliminated your competition and created a kingdom-wide demand for your unique, safer brand of magic.

The Art of the Master: Balancing the Brew

The amateur sees two separate forces: the good and the bad. The master sees one thing: the magnificent, terrifying, beautiful power of the unknown. The art of enterprise is not about choosing between playing it safe and taking a gamble. It is about understanding that they are one and the same.

The decision to pursue a radical new formula carries the downside risk of catastrophic failure and the upside risk of world-changing success. A true alchemist does not shy away from this. Instead, they honor both possibilities. They prepare for the worst, reinforcing the walls of the lab and keeping fire-suppressing powders at hand. But they also prepare for the best, ensuring they have enough vials to capture a miracle and the means to share it with the world.

This holistic view transforms risk management from a boring, defensive checklist into a dynamic, creative art form:

You become a Seer, scanning the stars not just for ill omens but for auspicious alignments.

You become a Master of Ingredients, understanding the dual nature of every element you handle—its potential to heal and its potential to harm.

You become a Composer, knowing when to stoke the flames to chase a brilliant new reaction, and when to cool the cauldron to maintain stability.

You build a Culture of Curiosity, empowering every apprentice to point out both cracks in the floor and strange, wonderful new colors in the brew.

Ultimately, the goal is not to avoid risk. The goal is to dance with it. It's to build an enterprise so resilient it can withstand the inevitable explosions, and so agile it can capture the fleeting sparks of genius. By respecting the shadows and chasing the light, we move beyond mere survival and begin the real work of the alchemist: turning the uncertainty of our world into the pure gold of lasting value.

Risks arising from internal and external sources

Forget the cold mechanics of a ship at sea. Let's think of an enterprise in a way that's far more intimate, more alive. Imagine it as a living, breathing being. It has a heart that pumps, a mind that thinks, a nervous system that fires with information, and a skin that separates it from the world. Like any living thing, its well-being is a delicate dance between its own internal health and the environment it inhabits. To truly understand risk is to understand this organism in its entirety—its vulnerabilities, its strengths, and its place in the wider ecosystem.

First, let's look inward, beneath the skin. This is the realm of self-inflicted wounds and chronic conditions, the risks born from the body's own composition.

At the very core, you have the human spirit—the soul of the operation. This is where the most profound potential and the most heartbreaking betrayals reside. People are not cogs; they are currents of ambition, fear, loyalty, and fallibility. A fraud isn't a line item; it's a story of a trusted individual succumbing to a private storm, tearing a hole in the fabric of the collective. It's a violation that poisons the trust that is the very oxygen of collaboration. But malice isn't the only threat. There's the simple, honest mistake—a tired mind, a slipped finger, a moment of distraction. A single misplaced decimal can become a tremor that cracks the foundation of a financial report. A culture of fear or insufficient training creates a kind of corporate anemia, where the workforce lacks the vitality and knowledge to perform, leading to clumsy errors and missed opportunities.

Then you have the body's essential systems—the operational rhythm. This is the circulatory system, the digestive tract, the very processes that turn intention into action. Today, the most critical of these is the digital nervous system. A cybersecurity breach isn't just a technical failure; it's a home invasion. Malicious code is a virus coursing through the veins, corrupting memory, stealing secrets, and holding the entire being for ransom. Think of the supply chain as the digestive system, taking in resources from the outside world. If a key supplier falters, it's like the body being starved of a vital nutrient, causing the entire organism to weaken and slow to a crawl. Inefficient internal processes are the clogged arteries of the business, slowing everything down, creating pressure, and threatening a catastrophic failure from a seemingly minor blockage.

The very skeleton of the enterprise—its technology—can become brittle with age. Outdated systems are like an old athlete's knees; they can function for a while, but they lack the agility for modern competition and are prone to sudden, painful failure. To refuse to evolve technologically is to willingly accept a competitive limp while others are learning to fly. And what of the lifeblood itself? The flow of capital. This is the enterprise's financial health. Poor planning isn't a spreadsheet error; it's a self-prescribed diet of junk food and adrenaline—a reckless pursuit of growth that leaves the body exhausted, over-leveraged, and vulnerable to the slightest shock.

Now, let's step outside. The world is not a sterile laboratory; it's a wilderness, beautiful and brutal. These are the external risks, the forces of nature and society that the enterprise must navigate.

The economic weather is always changing. A recession is a long, hard winter, forcing the organism to draw on its reserves, to hunker down and survive on less. Inflation is a fever that sweeps the land, making every resource more costly, every breath more difficult. Fluctuating currencies are like shifting gravitational fields, making every international step uncertain. These are conditions you don't control; you can only build a strong enough constitution to endure them.

The social and political terrain is constantly shifting underfoot. New regulations are not just legal text; they are new rules of physics for the environment. A new privacy law like GDPR is a fundamental change in how you must interact with the world, a new demand for respect and transparency. Political unrest in a foreign land is a sudden earthquake, sundering the supply lines you once relied upon. These are the powerful currents of the collective human ocean, and you are but one swimmer within them.

Out in the wilderness, you are not alone. There are other creatures, other competitors. The emergence of a disruptive startup isn't just a new company; it's a new species, evolved for the environment in a way you are not. It can outrun you, out-hunt you, and change the landscape forever. Think of the silence that fell over video rental stores as the sound of streaming began to hum. To ignore the competitive ecosystem is to become a dinosaur, gazing placidly at the approaching meteor.

And then there are the true bolts from the blue: the hurricanes, the floods, the pandemics. These are the moments the world itself seems to turn against you. A natural disaster doesn't check your balance sheet before it wipes your warehouse off the map. A global health crisis can instantly make your business model, your physical location, and your entire way of operating obsolete. These events remind us of our fragility, of the raw, unpredictable power of the planet we inhabit.

Finally, there is the risk of your story—your reputation. In our hyper-connected world, your identity is a fragile ghost, shaped by a million whispers on the wind. A single viral video, a poorly worded tweet, an exposed ethical lapse—it can all coalesce into a storm of public opinion that can shatter your good name overnight. Reputation is trust, and when it's gone, the world looks at you with different eyes.

So, what is the art of managing risk? It is the art of living wisely. It is nurturing a strong, healthy body—robust systems, a vibrant culture, a clear mind. It is also being a keen student of the world outside—watching the sky, reading the tracks, listening to the wind. It's not about building a fortress to keep the world out; that is a slow death. It's about cultivating the resilience of a seasoned trail runner, the adaptability of a creature that can thrive in sun or snow. It is a continuous, conscious act of balancing internal health with external reality, ensuring the enterprise doesn't just survive its journey, but becomes stronger, smarter, and more alive with every step it takes.

Risks arising from international operations

The Global Tightrope: Walking the Wire of International Business

Stepping onto the world stage feels like a grand opening. The spotlight is on, new audiences await, and the promise of growth is intoxicating. But what we often forget is that we're not stepping onto a wider stage, but onto a high-wire. The rewards on the other side are immense, but the air is thin, the winds are unpredictable, and there is no safety net unless you weave it yourself.

Venturing abroad isn't just about learning to say "hello" in a new language; it's about learning to read the silence, the weather, and the very ground beneath your feet. The risks aren't just line items in a report; they are living, breathing challenges that can make or break your global dream.

The Unwritten Rulebook and the Shifting Ground

Imagine playing a game where the rules change without notice, the referee favors the home team, and the field itself can tilt unexpectedly. That's the reality of navigating foreign political and economic landscapes.

The Political Quicksand: You might build your shiny new factory on what seems like solid ground, only to have a political tremor—a new election, a sudden policy reversal—turn that ground into quicksand. One day you're a valued investor; the next, your assets are being nationalized, or you're tangled in a web of new taxes designed to push you out. This isn't just business; it's political chess, and you need to be thinking several moves ahead, always asking, "What if?"

The Currency Casino: Your profit margins can feel like a gambler's lucky streak—entirely dependent on the volatile spin of the currency wheel. You earn in pesos, but you report in dollars. The peso dips, and suddenly your brilliant quarter is just... average. You can hedge, of course. You can buy financial instruments to protect yourself. But that's just another table in the casino, with its own costs and complexities. For example, if you expect to receive €1,000,000 in six months when the exchange rate is \$1.10/€, you budget for \$1,100,000. But if the euro weakens to \$1.03/€ by the payment date, your revenue shrinks to \$1,030,000—a \$70,000 loss born from a silent, invisible force.

The Human Element of Conflict: Beyond the balance sheets, there are people. Your people. In regions simmering with unrest, a protest or a conflict isn't a news headline; it's a direct threat to your team's safety and your company's ability to operate. Your contingency plan can't just be about rerouting shipments; it has to be about evacuating lives.

The Cultural Echo Chamber and the Web of Law

Success abroad is rarely about having the best product; it's about making the deepest connection. And that's where the most human risks lie.

Lost in Translation: The biggest barrier isn't language; it's context. A firm "yes" in one culture might mean "I hear you," not "I agree." A contract negotiation that feels aggressive in the West might be standard practice in the

East. These aren't quirks; they are the fundamental software of human interaction. If you fail to understand the local culture, you'll constantly be speaking into a void, your best intentions lost in a cultural echo chamber, leading to frustrated staff, alienated partners, and confused customers.

The Legal Labyrinth: Every country has its own maze of laws. What's a standard employee benefit at home could be illegal abroad. The data privacy measures that protect your customers in Europe are different from those in Asia. And what about your most precious asset—your idea? In some corners of the world, your patent might be seen as a suggestion, not a law. You could find your innovative product being sold by a counterfeiter on the very next street, a ghost of your own creation. Defending your intellectual property in a foreign court is a long, expensive, and lonely battle.

The Fragile Chain and the Whispers of Reputation

Your international operation is only as strong as its most fragile link. This chain stretches thousands of miles, across oceans and borders, and is exposed at every point.

The Tyranny of Distance: A port strike, a customs delay, a ship stuck in a canal—these are the logistical nightmares that can halt your entire business. A single storm can sever a critical link in your supply chain, leaving you with empty shelves and broken promises. Building redundancy and diversifying your supply lines isn't a luxury; it's your lifeline.

The Reputation That Travels at the Speed of Light: In our hyper-connected world, your reputation is your most valuable and most vulnerable asset. A misstep in a small, remote factory—an environmental accident, a report of poor labor conditions—doesn't stay local. It becomes a global headline in an instant. A single tweet can spark a boycott. A bad review can erode decades of brand loyalty. This is the ultimate risk, the one that encompasses all others. A political blunder, a cultural misreading, or a legal scandal all culminate here, in the court of public opinion, where trust, once lost, is nearly impossible to reclaim.

Weaving your own safety net means seeing these risks not as threats to be avoided, but as challenges to be understood. It requires more than financial acumen; it demands cultural curiosity, ethical courage, and a deep-seated humility. The global tightrope is daunting, but for those who learn to balance, to adapt to the winds, and to respect the wire they walk upon, the view from the other side is truly limitless.

Strategic and operational risks

Of Pulse and Peril: A Guide to the Lifeblood of Your Business

Every enterprise has a heartbeat. A rhythm of daily tasks, monthly reports, and quarterly goals. It has a brain—the C-suite—that dreams, plans, and sets a course for the future. And it has a soul: its purpose, its brand, its reason for being. But like any living thing, it's also vulnerable. It faces the sudden, existential threat of a changing world and the slow, internal decay of its own systems. These are the two fundamental forces of uncertainty every leader must wrestle with: the strategic and the operational.

Forget dusty textbooks and sterile flowcharts for a moment. Think of your organization as a living, breathing entity. Understanding risk is not about managing a list; it's about practicing medicine. It's about being a doctor to your own enterprise, checking its vitals, diagnosing its illnesses, and nurturing it toward a long and vibrant life.

The Existential Ache: Confronting Strategic Sickness

Strategic risks are the chronic, congenital, and environmental diseases that can threaten the very life of your corporate body. They don't just cause a bad quarter; they challenge your right to exist in the next decade. They are the slow-moving but unstoppable forces that demand you evolve or perish.

Imagine the "ecosystem collapse" of market disruption. You are a mighty woolly mammoth, perfectly adapted to the Ice Age. Your strength is legendary. But the climate is changing. The glaciers are retreating, the grasslands are turning to forests, and smaller, faster mammals are thriving. Your entire world is shifting, and your very design is becoming a liability. This was the fate of Blockbuster watching the warm winds of streaming services melt its icy empire. It's not a business problem; it's an evolutionary one.

Then there is the "sudden environmental toxicity" of political and regulatory shifts. Your organization is a thriving coral reef, a complex and beautiful ecosystem. Suddenly, a new law—a chemical spill of tariffs, a change in environmental policy—alters the very chemistry of the water. The cost of survival skyrockets, and parts of your beautiful reef may begin to bleach and die. This is the vertigo felt by companies caught in the crosscurrents of trade wars or blindsided by new compliance mandates.

Consider the "creeping genetic obsolescence" of technology. The DNA of your business—its core processes, its tools, its customer interfaces—is what makes it work. But the world is constantly sequencing new, more efficient

DNA. If you fail to splice in new technological advancements, you risk becoming a relic, out-competed by organisms that are faster, smarter, and better adapted to the digital landscape. Your analog heart can't pump blood fast enough for a high-speed world.

And what of reputational damage? This is a "disease of the soul." In a hyper-connected world, your company's character is its immune system. A single scandal, a viral misstep, an ethical lapse—it's a fast-acting virus that can ravage your public image. It doesn't just hurt sales; it creates a deep-seated distrust that makes it hard to attract talent, partners, and customers. It's the corporate equivalent of losing the will to live.

The Daily Grind: Healing Operational Ailments

If strategic risks are chronic diseases, operational risks are the acute illnesses, the broken bones, and the infections of the daily grind. They are the thousand small ways the body can fail itself. Ignored, these seemingly minor ailments can fester, leading to systemic failure and leaving the body vulnerable to those larger, strategic threats.

Think of process failures as "clogged arteries or misfiring synapses." The brain (strategy) sends a signal: "Invoice the client." But somewhere in the nervous system of your operations, the message is lost, garbled, or sent to the wrong limb. The invoice is wrong, the product is mislabeled, the customer is forgotten. Each one is a small stroke, a minor pain, but their cumulative effect is a slow, creeping paralysis of inefficiency and frustration.

System and technology failures are the body's "seizures or massive organ failures." Your IT infrastructure is the central nervous system. When it crashes, the entire body goes limp. A server outage is a heart attack. A data breach is a hemorrhagic stroke, leaking your most vital lifeblood—your data—out into the world. In this state, the body isn't just inefficient; it's completely vulnerable, lying comatose as predators circle.

Human error and internal fraud represent an "autoimmune disease." This is when the body turns on itself. Sometimes it's unintentional—a cell that doesn't replicate correctly, a well-meaning hand that slips. But sometimes it's more sinister. Fraud is a cancer, a cell that decides to work only for itself, draining resources and poisoning the host from within for its own gain. It's a profound betrayal of the body's own biology.

Supply chain disruptions are a form of "acute malnutrition or circulatory blockage." Your business can't get the nutrients it needs to function. A supplier fails, a port closes, a truck stops running. The limbs—your factories and storefronts—begin to starve for inventory. The whole body weakens, unable to perform even the most basic functions.

The Mind-Body Connection: A Holistic Diagnosis

Here is the essential truth: you cannot treat the soul without treating the body. The strategic and the operational are not separate. They are inextricably linked in a delicate mind-body connection.

A strategic decision to run a marathon (enter a new market) puts immense stress on the body's operational muscles, lungs, and heart. If those systems aren't prepared, the body will break down long before the finish line. Conversely, a chronic operational ailment—a nagging pain from a process failure, a constant infection from poor security—drains the body's energy and morale. This constant pain distracts the brain, making it impossible to think clearly about the future. A body in constant, operational pain loses its strategic ambition.

True enterprise resilience, then, is a form of holistic wellness. It's about building a strong operational body—with clean processes, robust systems, and a healthy culture—so that it can support the ambitious dreams of the strategic mind. It's about fostering a risk-aware culture that acts as the body's immune system, constantly seeking out and neutralizing threats, big and small.

By viewing your enterprise not as a machine to be managed, but as a life to be nurtured, you move beyond the sterile language of risk mitigation. You begin the essential, human work of building an organization that doesn't just survive uncertainty, but is resilient enough to thrive in it.

Explanatory notes

What are the types and sources of risks that would prevent organisations from implementing their intended strategy?

Every great strategy begins as a beautiful map. It's a vision of a distant shore—a treasure island of market dominance, innovation, and success. The leadership team unfurls it in the boardroom, pointing to the X that marks the spot. The path looks clear, the journey exciting.

But between the drawing board and the destination lies the vast, unpredictable ocean of reality. And this ocean is filled with ghosts. It's a graveyard of brilliant plans and beautiful maps, all sunk by the hidden reefs, sudden storms, and sea monsters they failed to anticipate. These are the risks that haunt the voyage from idea to implementation. To navigate these waters, you must first learn to see them, not as items on a spreadsheet, but as the living, breathing challenges they are.

The Phantom Reefs: When the Map Itself is Wrong (Strategic Risks)

Sometimes, the danger isn't in the ocean, but in the chart room. The map you're holding might be leading you directly into peril.

A Map to Nowhere: The most tragic failure is a flawlessly executed journey to the wrong place. This happens when the strategy is born from a delusion—a misreading of the currents of the market, a hubris about the ship's own speed and strength, or a blind spot for the rocks just below the surface. If your core assumptions are flawed, every gust of wind in your sails only pushes you faster towards disaster.

The Shifting Tides: You might have the perfect map for yesterday's ocean. But the world doesn't sit still. Consumer desires drift like migrating currents, new technologies surface like volcanic islands, and disruptive business models can appear overnight, changing the very shape of the coastline. Blockbuster had a masterful map of the video rental world, but they never saw the continent of streaming rise from the sea, making their entire world obsolete.

Rival Captains and Pirate Ships: You are not the only ship on the sea. Other captains are watching you. They're faster, more cunning, or they've just invented a new kind of sail. A strategy that doesn't obsessively watch the horizon for these rival vessels—or the sudden appearance of a small, fast pirate ship (a startup) that can outmaneuver you—will find its treasure stolen before it even gets there.

The Kraken of Technology: Deep in the waters, technological monsters sleep. When they awaken, they can capsize entire fleets. Artificial intelligence, quantum computing, biotechnology—these are the krakens of our time. To ignore their tremors is to sail with a foolish confidence, unaware that the world beneath you is about to be completely rewritten.

The Laws of the Sea: The seas are governed by powerful, unseen forces—regulations, political squalls, and trade wars. A shift in international policy can close a vital shipping lane overnight. New environmental laws can demand you rebuild your engine mid-voyage. A strategy that ignores the political climate is like a ship sailing into a naval blockade, armed with nothing but a hopeful map.

The Creaking Hull: When the Ship is Unseaworthy (Operational Risks)

Even with a perfect map, a ship can be its own worst enemy. The real struggle is often fought on your own decks, with your own crew and equipment.

A Crew of Landlubbers (People Risk): A voyage to a new world requires new skills. You can't navigate treacherous straits if your crew has never handled a tiller. A skills gap in your workforce is a quiet but deadly threat. Worse yet is mutiny. When a crew fears the new direction, doesn't understand the captain's orders, or feels their future is threatened, they won't just work poorly—they may actively saw through the floorboards. Without clear communication and a shared sense of purpose, the whispers of resistance below deck will sink you faster than any storm.

Tangled Rigging and Ropes (Process Risk): Imagine trying to hoist the sails, but all the ropes are hopelessly knotted. This is what happens when a futuristic strategy is forced through archaic internal processes. If your systems for getting things done are slow, convoluted, and lack clear ownership, your grand voyage will stall in the harbor, tangled in its own bureaucracy.

A Leaky Hull and Rusted Compass (Systems & Technology Risk): Your IT systems are the hull of your ship; your data is the compass. If your hull is a patchwork of legacy systems, it will spring leaks under the pressure of a new journey. If it's not protected, cyber-pirates will breach it, stealing your cargo (data) and your reputation. And if your compass (your data) is faulty, you're not navigating; you're just lost.

Empty Barrels: When the Supplies Run Out (Financial Risks)

A ship can't sail on courage alone. It needs provisions. Money is the food and water for your strategic journey.

Not Enough Rations for the Voyage: The most common reason ships turn back is that they simply run out of supplies. Ambitious strategies are hungry. They devour capital for research, marketing, and talent. Underestimate the cost, and you'll find your crew starving and your voyage abandoned halfway to the destination.

The Stores are Spoiling: It's not just about how much food you have, but whether it's accessible. Cash flow problems are like rot spreading through your provisions. Even with a hold full of assets, if you can't pay the crew their wages tomorrow, a mutiny is brewing.

The Perfect Storm: When Everything Happens at Once

These risks are not polite; they don't take turns. They are interconnected and love to gang up on you. A sudden geopolitical squall (External Risk) strains your supply lines (Operational Risk), leading to cost overruns (Financial Risk). This forces you to cut your cybersecurity budget (Operational Risk), which allows a pirate attack that damages your reputation (Strategic Risk), causing your best sailors to abandon ship. This is the perfect storm, where one vulnerability triggers a cascade that brings the entire enterprise down.

To truly succeed, you must do more than just draw a beautiful map. You must become a master mariner. This means fostering a crew that is resilient, adaptable, and constantly scanning the horizon. It means building a ship that is not just strong, but flexible enough to ride the waves. It means knowing that the ocean will always be unpredictable, and that the true art of strategy lies not in having a perfect plan, but in the courage and skill to navigate the journey, no matter what monsters rise from the deep.

Evaluate Risk

Evaluate the impact of risk

The Unseen Architecture of Risk: A Story of a Company's Soul

We try to cage it in spreadsheets, to tame it with algorithms, and to predict its path with elegant charts. We call it "risk," a clinical, one-syllable word for a force as wild and ancient as human ambition itself. But the true story of risk isn't told in the cold math of a balance sheet; it's written in the invisible ink of human experience. It's a story that unfolds not in boardrooms alone, but in the quiet corridors of a company, in the hearts of its people, and in the echo it leaves on the world.

The Ghost in the Machine

When disaster strikes—a data breach, a product failure, a PR nightmare—the first tremor we feel is financial. It's the easiest to measure, the starkest number. But this is merely the shockwave. The real damage, the lingering haunt, is far more subtle. It's the ghost of doubt that begins to haunt the hallways.

Trust, that sacred, invisible bond between a company and its customers, doesn't break; it evaporates. It becomes a coolness in conversations, a hesitation before purchase, a story whispered from one friend to another. This isn't a line item on a budget; it's the slow hollowing out of a brand's soul. Inside the walls, the same chill spreads. The unspoken fear of layoffs after a scandal, the dip in pride when the company's name becomes a punchline—these are the human costs. They manifest as a quiet retreat into self-preservation, where innovation is shelved, and brilliance is muffled for fear of misstep. The most talented people don't always leave loudly; they just stop bringing their whole selves to work.

And what of reputation? In our hyper-connected world, reputation is no longer a monument built of stone; it's a story told about you when you're not in the room, a digital wildfire that can be sparked by a single tweet. Rebuilding it is not a matter of issuing a press release. It's a painstaking act of reconciliation, an often-impossible quest to win back the public's heart, one person at a time. The real impact is the loss of a narrative, the forfeiture of the right to tell your own story.

The Human Tremor

Beyond the institution, risk is an intensely personal affair. It's the solitary weight on a leader's shoulders in a 3 AM crisis, grappling with decisions that will define careers and lives, with nothing but incomplete data and their own gut for a guide. The burnout from this constant state of high alert is a silent epidemic, draining the very creativity and courage that leadership demands.

For every person on the team, a high-risk environment can feel like walking on perpetually shifting ground. It frays the social fabric that turns a group of employees into a community. Communication breaks down into whispers, collaboration gives way to suspicion, and the shared sense of purpose dissolves into individual anxiety.

This human tremor extends far beyond the company's walls. A factory spill isn't just a clean-up cost and a regulatory fine; it's a scar on the land, a story of loss etched into a community's memory for generations. The true impact is measured in the health of a river, the trust of a town, and the fundamental question of a company's right to operate. It asks a profound question: What is our legacy beyond profit?

The Crossroads of Fear and Fortune

To see risk only as a monster to be slain is to miss its other face: that of the catalyst. A human-centric view understands that risk is the price of admission for anything worthwhile. It's the trembling uncertainty before a great leap. This presents a fundamental choice: do we build a fortress or a vessel?

A fortress is built to keep risk out. It is safe, predictable, and unchanging. But it is also a prison. Nothing new gets in, and no great expeditions can ever leave. A vessel, however, is built for the journey. It embraces the uncertainty of the sea, designed not to avoid storms but to navigate them. An organization that learns to manage risk like a skilled sailor—reading the winds, mending the sails, and trusting the crew—can discover new worlds of opportunity that the fortress-dwellers will never know.

This creates resilience, which is not a plan, but a culture. It is the muscle memory for crisis, the shared instinct that kicks in when things go wrong. A resilient organization doesn't just survive the storm; it is forged by it, emerging with a deeper understanding of its own strength and a renewed sense of purpose.

Whispers of the Future

The landscape of risk is not a map; it is a living, breathing climate, constantly changing. The digital specter of a cyberattack, a war waged in whispers of code, can now cripple a nation. The slow, undeniable rewriting of our planet's rules by climate change threatens to upend supply chains and redraw coastlines.

To navigate this future, we need more than better technology. We need to turn every employee into a sensor, a human antenna attuned to the subtle shifts in the environment. We need to foster a culture where a concern from the front lines is treated with the same gravity as a report from the C-suite. This collective intelligence, this organizational nervous system, is our only true guide through the uncharted territories ahead.

In the end, how we approach risk is the ultimate reflection of our values. It reveals what we are willing to protect, what we dare to reach for, and who we choose to be when the predictable world falls away. It is more than a strategy; it is the human signature we leave on the world.

Assess the likelihood of risks

The Cartographer's Art: Mapping the Fog of Business Risk

Forget the spreadsheets for a moment. Forget the sterile language of "mitigation" and "quantitative analysis." Let's talk about what it really means to stare into the future of your business. It's not about predicting a single, certain fate with a crystal ball. It's about being a cartographer of the unseen, a scout sent into the misty landscape of tomorrow to map its terrain—its hidden pits, its sudden cliffs, and its unexpected safe harbors.

Assessing the "likelihood" of a risk is the heart of this modern map-making. It's the art of listening to the wind, reading the tracks in the soil, and translating that wisdom into a guide that lets us navigate the unknown not with fear, but with a quiet, prepared confidence. Without this map, we're simply wandering, hoping for the best. With it, we can choose our path, brace for storms, and even find opportunities where others only see shadows.

Reading the Landscape of Likelihood

To draw this map, a great cartographer relies on more than one tool. The landscape of risk is shaped by forces both ancient and immediate, both seen and unseen.

First, you look at the old maps and journals. This is your historical data. Where have past expeditions—in your company, in your industry—stumbled? The records of old data breaches are like skulls marking a poisoned well. The patterns of past supply chain collapses are the warnings of a seasonal monsoon. These histories don't dictate the future, but they whisper powerful warnings about the nature of the terrain you're about to cross.

Next, you talk to the seasoned local guides. This is your expert judgment. These are the people with dirt under their fingernails—the grizzled engineer who knows the sound a machine makes just before it fails, the savvy marketer who can feel a shift in public mood long before the sales data confirms it. Their intuition, honed over years of experience, provides the nuanced detail that raw data can never capture. They know the shortcuts, the local customs, and the places where dragons lie.

Then, you must constantly scan the horizon for the changing weather. These are your external factors. A geopolitical storm brewing a thousand miles away can send a flash flood of disruption down your valley. A technological earthquake can change the very landscape overnight. A good scout doesn't just watch their feet; they watch the sky, read the atmospheric pressure of global markets, and feel the tectonic shifts of innovation.

And you can't forget to check the sturdiness of your own expedition team. These are your internal factors. How strong are your shelters (internal controls)? Is your team communicating clearly, or is there dissent and confusion (organizational culture)? A well-equipped, disciplined, and resilient team can navigate a treacherous path with grace. A weak one can turn a minor stumble into a full-blown catastrophe.

Finally, you must see the web of connections. A risk is rarely a solo predator. It moves in packs. A loose rock (a minor cyber event) starts a small landslide (a data leak), which dislodges a boulder (reputational damage), which triggers an avalanche (regulatory fines and class-action lawsuits). A true master cartographer doesn't just map individual hazards; they map the chain reactions, understanding how one event can wake a dozen sleeping dangers.

Sketching vs. Surveying: Two Ways to Draw the Map

How do you mark these dangers on your map? You have two primary methods, each with its own soul.

Qualitative mapping is the art of the sketch. It's intuitive, fast, and visceral. You use words that carry weight: "treacherous pass," "unlikely oasis," "almost certain ambush." This is the language of the scout, relying on experience and gut feeling. It's powerful because it's human. We understand what "treacherous" feels like. The challenge is that one person's "treacherous" is another's "challenging." Clear legends are needed, so everyone knows exactly what the sketch artist meant.

Quantitative mapping, by contrast, is the work of the surveyor with their precise instruments. It replaces sketches with hard numbers: "a 20% chance of rockfall in this canyon," "an ambush occurs here once every five years." This method brings a beautiful, cold clarity. It's perfect for well-trodden paths where you have lots of data. But it can create a dangerous illusion of certainty. After all, your instruments are only as good as your understanding of the landscape, and sometimes, the ground itself is new and unmeasurable.

The wisest cartographers use both. They use the intuitive sketch to identify the most dangerous regions, and then they bring in the surveyor's tools to measure them with precision.

The Never-Ending Journey

Making this map is not a one-time act. It's a living, breathing process. The landscape of business is dynamic; mountains rise, rivers change course. The map you drew yesterday might be dangerously out of date by tomorrow. The journey requires constant vigilance:

Spotting the Shadows: Actively searching the horizon for new shapes that might be threats.

Gathering Intelligence: Talking to other travelers, studying the terrain, listening to the whispers on the wind.

Marking the Map: Making the bold, decisive mark—qualitative or quantitative—that says, "Here lies a danger."

Logging the Journey: Keeping a clear record of why you marked the map as you did, so those who follow can learn from your journey.

Re-surveying Relentlessly: Recognizing that the map is never finished. You must constantly be looking at the world with fresh eyes.

This journey is fraught with its own perils—the mirage of optimism that makes us underestimate danger, the echo chamber of our own team that confirms our biases, and the sheer speed at which the world changes.

But a precise, living map of likelihood does more than just help us dodge bullets. It transforms our entire enterprise. It tells us where to build our fortresses (resource allocation), which paths are worth the risk (strategic decisions), and what supplies to carry for the journey ahead (contingency planning).

Ultimately, assessing likelihood is about trading fear of the unknown for a deep respect for it. It empowers us to step into the fog not with blind faith, but with the best map human ingenuity can create—a map that gives us the courage to be bold, the wisdom to be prudent, and the foresight to build an enterprise that can thrive in any landscape.

Analyse the interaction of different risks

The Secret Life of Risk: A Ghost Story for the Modern Enterprise

Let's be honest. We like to think of our businesses as well-oiled machines. Predictable, logical, controllable. We draw neat org charts and build tidy spreadsheets, creating a comforting illusion of order. But that's not the truth, is it?

The truth is, an enterprise isn't a machine. It's a living, breathing organism. And like any organism, it has a shadow self—a complex, invisible ecosystem of risks that live in the walls, whisper in the server rooms, and travel along the supply chains. We give them sterile names:

operational risk, financial risk, strategic risk. We put them in separate boxes, hoping to contain them.

But they don't stay in their boxes. They talk to each other. They conspire. They breed. And the sound of their interaction isn't a gentle hum; it's the discordant music of a gathering storm. Ignoring this secret life, this ghost in our machine, isn't just bad practice. It's an invitation to disaster.

The First Domino: When a Whisper Becomes a Scream

It often starts with a single, quiet event. A tremor. A new government regulation is passed—a headache for the legal team, certainly, but seemingly contained. We label it "compliance risk" and file it away. But the whisper has already started its journey.

The legal team sends a panicked memo: we need new systems, new training, now. The whisper reaches the finance department, which now sees a budget bleeding cash to pay for this unexpected overhaul. This is a "financial risk." To cover the cost, they freeze hiring and delay equipment upgrades. Now the whisper is in operations, where overworked teams and aging infrastructure start to groan under the strain. An "operational risk" is born. That single, quiet tremor—that one domino—has sent a shockwave through the entire body of the company, leaving a trail of new, angry risks in its wake.

The Feedback Loop from Hell: How Risks Feed Each Other

Some risks don't just trigger others; they form a toxic partnership, creating a feedback loop that spirals out of control. Imagine your company is carrying a heavy backpack of debt. It's a manageable weight, a calculated "financial risk." Now, imagine the ground beneath your feet begins to tremble—a market downturn, another "financial risk."

Separately, you could handle either. But together? The downturn shrinks your revenue, making the backpack of debt feel impossibly heavy. To service the debt, you cut deeper, slashing the very muscle you need to climb out of the downturn. The debt feeds the weakness, and the weakness feeds the debt. It's a vicious, self-perpetuating cycle where 1+1 doesn't equal 2, it equals a catastrophe. This is how a company drowns, not in a single wave, but in the churning vortex created by two forces pulling it under at once.

The Unseen Bullseye: Where Dangers Quietly Converge

Sometimes, these whispering risks aren't spread out. They're all staring at the same single point of failure—an unseen bullseye painted on a critical part of your business. You might think you have a dozen different suppliers, but what if they all rely on a single port for shipping? Or a single software for logistics?

The most classic bullseye is the "golden supplier"—that one partner who provides a component so essential, they are practically the aorta of your operations. You've identified a "supply chain risk," but what you really have is a massive concentration of risk. If a fire, a flood, or a political crisis hits that one supplier, it's not a disruption. It's a corporate heart attack. Your "operational risk" of a factory shutdown is triggered instantly. Your "financial risk" explodes as orders go unfulfilled. Your "reputation risk" skyrockets as you break promises to customers. All because dozens of hidden risk pathways led back to one single, vulnerable point.

The Meltdown: When the Whole System Catches Fire

This is the ultimate horror story. This is the cascading failure. It's the moment the interconnectedness of risk becomes terrifyingly clear, like watching a single spark leap from a frayed wire to an oil slick, to the whole damn building.

Think of a cyberattack. It starts as a "cybersecurity risk." But it's not just about data. The attack cripples your central IT system—a digital stroke that paralyzes the company. Your "operational risk" ignites as manufacturing lines halt. Your "logistical risk" flares up as trucks can't be dispatched. Your "legal risk" explodes as you begin breaching contracts with every passing hour. Your "reputation risk" goes supernova as the world watches your company grind to a halt.

This isn't a series of individual problems. It's a single, unfolding event of systemic collapse. The failure of one system didn't just cause the failure of the next; it poured gasoline on it.

Learning to Hear the Whispers: How to Survive the Ghost Story

So, what do we do? We can't exorcise these ghosts. Risk is a fundamental part of existence. But we can learn to listen to them. We can become risk whisperers.

It starts by admitting our neat boxes are a fantasy. We need to get people from finance, legal, operations, and IT in the same room, not to talk about their risks, but to talk about our risks. We need to tell scary stories—running scenarios and stress tests that are deliberately cruel, combining a supply shock with a social media crisis, or a currency collapse with a product recall.

It means building in shock absorbers. Not just a backup supplier, but two or three. Not just one server farm, but a decentralized network. It means creating a culture where the person on the factory floor feels just as responsible for spotting a strange tremor as the CFO.

Ultimately, navigating this world is not about building higher walls. It's about understanding the secret architecture of how things connect. It's about appreciating that the most dangerous threats aren't the loud monsters you see coming, but the silent, interconnected network of whispers you never thought to listen for. The goal isn't to silence the ghosts in the machine; it's to learn their language.

Quantification of risk exposure

Of Ghosts and Balance Sheets: Learning to See the Risks You Can't Touch

Every business, from the garage-born dream to the glass-towered giant, is a haunted house. It's built on a foundation of ambition, but its hallways echo with the whispers of what-ifs. These are the phantoms of risk—the specters of market crashes, the ghosts of supply chain failures, the poltergeists of public relations disasters. They are unseen, unnerving, and they have the power to turn a thriving enterprise into a cautionary tale.

To simply live in this haunted house, knocking on wood and hoping for the best, is not a strategy; it's a surrender. The modern leader can't just be a resident; they must become a paranormal investigator. The goal isn't to exorcise every spirit—an impossible and frankly, boring ambition—but to map the cold spots, to measure the whispers, and to understand the unseen forces at play. This is the art and science of quantifying risk: turning a gut feeling into a blueprint, and fear into foresight.

Why We Learn to Speak with Phantoms

Wrestling with numbers to define something as slippery as risk can feel like trying to catch smoke in a net. But the alternative is to be perpetually at the mercy of shadows. When we give risk a number, we give it a name, and a named thing is a thing we can face.

It Creates a Common Tongue. Imagine trying to warn a skeptic about a ghost. "I feel a dark presence in the server room!" you might say. They'll likely offer you a cup of coffee. But if you can say, "There is a 15% chance of a server failure in the next quarter, which translates to a probable loss of $1.2 million in sales and recovery costs," you are no longer speaking in tongues. You are speaking the universal language of the balance sheet. Suddenly, everyone from IT to the C-suite is listening, ready to help reinforce the door.

It Tells You Which Monsters to Fight First. Not all bumps in the night are created equal. Is that a mouse in the wall or a dragon in the basement? Without measurement, we often waste our energy on the loudest, but not necessarily the most dangerous, threats. By assigning a value—a weight, a temperature, a cost—to each risk, we can create a hierarchy of horrors. It allows us to focus our silver bullets not on the noisy ghouls, but on the silent, smiling specters with the power to truly bring the house down.

It Turns Gambles into Calculated Journeys. Should we open the door to that new, treasure-filled wing of the house, knowing it's rumored to be the most haunted? Without data, the decision is a coin flip in the dark. But with a quantified map of the risks, we can weigh the potential treasure against the measured threat. The decision transforms from a blind leap of faith into a strategic step, taken with eyes wide open, fully aware of the potential cost of the ghosts you might awaken.

It Builds a Fortress of Trust. In a world of uncertainty, those who can demonstrate mastery over their own phantoms command respect. Investors, regulators, and partners aren't looking for a business with no risks; they are looking for a business that understands its risks intimately. A quantified, rigorous approach to risk is a signal of sophisticated governance. It's the ultimate proof that you are not just living in the haunted house—you are the warden, in control, with the lights on and a plan for whatever goes bump in the night.

The Investigator's Toolkit: Instruments for Seeing the Unseen

To measure a phantom, you need more than courage; you need specialized equipment. Each tool gives you a different reading, a different glimpse into the ethereal plane of probability and impact.

A foundational tool is the Séance of Statistics, more formally known as Expected Loss Calculation. It's a direct conversation with a specific risk. You multiply the probability of the spirit manifesting (P) by the cost of the havoc it will wreak if it does (I).
$E(L)=P\times I$

If there's a 5% chance (P=0.05) of a data breach that would cost $4 million to clean up ($I=$4,000,000), the expected loss, or the "ghostly presence" on your budget, is $200,000. It's simple, powerful, but its clarity depends entirely on how well you can estimate the odds and the impact.

For more complex hauntings, investigators use a Full-Spectrum Ectoplasmic Analysis, or Monte Carlo Simulation. Instead of one number for probability and one for impact, you feed the machine a whole range of possibilities for dozens of variables—interest rates, customer churn, shipping delays. The simulation then runs thousands, even millions, of possible futures, like playing out every possible path the ghost could take through the house. The result isn't a single number, but a rich tapestry of potential outcomes, showing you the most likely financial picture and the terrifying, but rare, worst-case scenarios.

In the world of market risk, many rely on a Containment Field known as Value at Risk (VaR). VaR doesn't tell you what will happen; it draws a line in the sand. A one-day VaR of $5 million at 95% confidence says, "On 19 out of 20 days, we are confident we won't lose more than $5 million." It's a powerful shield, but its great weakness is what lies beyond that line—the 1-in-20 day, the "tail event," when the monster breaks the containment field entirely.

And for the creaks and groans of daily operations, there's Failure Mode and Effects Analysis (FMEA). Think of it as placing microphones all over the house to listen for the faintest signs of stress. By scoring the Severity, Occurrence, and Detectability of tiny potential failures, you can calculate a Risk Priority Number (RPN) to find and fix the weakest floorboards before they give way.

The Human Fog: When Our Own Ghosts Cloud the Numbers

Here lies the investigator's paradox: the greatest source of distortion isn't the phantom, but the person holding the equipment. Numbers feel objective, but they are born from human assumptions, and humans are notoriously unreliable narrators.

The first challenge is a Static-Filled Signal, or poor data. For new, strange risks—the kind we've never seen before—we have no historical record. We are forced to rely on expert guesses and industry whispers, which can be as unreliable as a foggy crystal ball.

Then there is the Unmeasurable Chill. How do you assign a dollar value to a shattered reputation? To the slow drain of employee morale? To the loss of a customer's trust? These are the most profound impacts, the deep, existential dread that a haunting leaves behind, and they often defy quantification.

Worst of all is the Hubris of the Hunter. A dashboard full of neat numbers and green-lit charts can create a dangerous illusion of control. We can become so mesmerized by our own tools that we forget they are just models of reality, not reality itself. We trust the readout from our ghost meter while ignoring the blood-curdling scream from the next room.

The Vigil Never Ends

Quantifying risk is not a one-time exorcism. It is a perpetual vigil. The architecture of your business changes, new doors open, old spirits fade, and new ones are born in the shadows of new technology and new markets. Your models must be constantly challenged, your data refreshed, and your assumptions questioned.

Ultimately, giving numbers to your risks is an act of profound creativity and courage. It's an admission that you can't control the world, but a declaration that you will not be a victim of its uncertainties. It's about switching on the lights, not to banish the ghosts, but to see them clearly, to learn their names, and to find the courage to lead, not in spite of them, but alongside them. It is how we learn to master the haunted, beautiful, and ultimately rewarding house we call our business.

Risk maps

Charting the Corporate Sea: Why Your Business Needs a Ghost Map for Risk

Every business is a ship at sea. Whether you're a scrappy startup in a dinghy or a multinational conglomerate commanding a fleet, you're navigating. And the waters of commerce are notoriously treacherous, filled with sudden squalls of market volatility, the jagged reefs of regulatory change, and the deep, unseen leviathans of systemic failure. To sail blind is not bravery; it's an invitation to disaster. You need a chart. Not just any chart, but one that maps the ghosts—a risk map.

A risk map isn't a spreadsheet disguised with color. It's a truth-teller. It's a visual conversation about what could go wrong, cutting through the noise and corporate jargon to show you exactly where the monsters lie. In the world of enterprise risk, and for the strategic minds pursuing a CGMA designation, learning to read and draw these maps is the difference between being a passenger and being the master navigator of your vessel.

Seeing the Unseen: The Anatomy of a Ghost Map

Forget sterile grids and axes for a moment. Think of it this way: a risk map asks two beautifully simple, terrifyingly important questions.

"How likely is this ghost to show up?" (This is your likelihood.)

"If it does, how bad will the haunting be?" (This is your impact.)

By plotting the answers, you create a supernatural sonar screen for your company. The minor gremlins that might trip a wire but cause little fuss? They float in the calm, green-tinted waters in the bottom-left corner. But the potential company-sinking krakens—the high-likelihood, high-impact terrors—they flash a brilliant, urgent red in the top-right. They demand your attention, your resources, your best monster-hunters.

This single picture does what a hundred-page report cannot: it tells a story. It provides a shared vision of the battlefield, allowing everyone from the engine room to the bridge to understand the dangers in a single, gut-level glance.

More Than a Pretty Picture: The Navigator's Edge

Why is this simple drawing so revolutionary? Because it changes the entire posture of an organization from reactive to clairvoyant.

First, it banishes indecision. Resources are your crew's energy, your capital, your time. They are finite. Without a map, you might waste them chasing phantom lights while a real threat looms off the port bow. A risk map forces focus. It shines a spotlight on the few critical threats that truly matter, guiding your cannons to where they'll have the most devastatingly protective effect.

Second, it builds a unified crew. Try explaining a dense risk register to your board of directors. You'll see their eyes glaze over. Now, show them a heatmap where a massive red blotch labeled "Supply Chain Collapse" is pulsing ominously. Suddenly, you have their undivided attention. The map becomes a campfire, a central point for discussion, debate, and collaboration. It dissolves departmental silos and turns a collection of individuals into a single, risk-aware crew, all reading from the same cursed—and vital—scroll.

Third, it's a living oracle. The sea is never static. That dormant volcano on the horizon? It might start smoking. A risk map is not a one-time sketch to be framed and forgotten; it's the ship's living logbook. By revisiting it, updating it, watching the ghosts shift and morph, you can track the changing weather of your risk profile. It becomes a rhythmic pulse check on the organization's health, allowing you to adjust your course long before the storm hits.

Finally, it makes you a bolder explorer. True navigation isn't just about avoiding reefs; it's about confidently charting a course to new worlds—new markets, new products, new ventures. By mapping the dangers inherent in a new strategy, you can weigh the treasure against the dragons. It transforms risk from a paralyzing specter into a calculated variable, allowing for smarter, braver, and ultimately more rewarding expeditions.

The Ritual of Creation: Summoning Your Map

A truly powerful map isn't just drawn; it's summoned through a careful, collaborative ritual.

It begins with a séance to identify the spirits. This is a company-wide ghost hunt. Through workshops, interviews, and deep dives into data, you must give a name to every fear, every potential gremlin and ghoul that could sabotage your journey.

Next, you weigh each ghost's power. For every risk identified, you must assess its likelihood (the chances it will manifest) and its impact (the scale of the wreckage if it does). This isn't just about financial cost; it's about the damage to your name, the disruption to your people, the wrath of the regulators. This is where you plot the inherent risk—the monster in its raw, untamed form.

Then comes the most strategic conversation: defining your courage. This is your risk appetite. How much danger are you willing to accept to achieve your goals? Where do you draw the line between a thrilling adventure and a suicide mission? This defines your red zone and tells you which ghosts you simply cannot tolerate.

Finally, you assess your defenses to reveal the residual risk. You have alarms, stronger hulls, and seasoned monster-slayers (your controls and mitigation plans). How effective are they? The risk that remains after these defenses are accounted for is your residual risk. This is the haunting you actually live with day-to-day. The goal of all your hard work is to drag the terrifying red-zone threats down into the manageable green, taming the beasts that prowl your waters.

Beyond the Basic Compass

The art of map-making is evolving. Some navigators now use 5x5 grids for more nuance. Others add a third dimension, like velocity—how fast the monster swims towards you—or a fourth, controllability, turning their flat chart into a holographic command center. The best format is the one your crew understands and uses to make better decisions.

But beware the navigator's sins. The Sin of the Dusty Map, left in a drawer to become obsolete. The Sin of Over-Charting, where you map every minnow and lose sight of the sharks. And the worst sin of all: Checkbox Cartography, creating a map just to prove you have one, without letting it guide a single decision. A risk map must be a living tool, its edges worn from constant use.

For the CGMA professional, this is not just a skill; it is the essence of your role. You are the First Mate, the Master Navigator. It is your job to create the map, to interpret its whispers and warnings, and to translate its cryptic symbols into a clear plan of action for your captain and crew.

A risk map is not the end of the journey. It is the beginning of a wiser one. It's the confidence to know that while the sea will always be unpredictable, you are no longer sailing blind. You have your chart, you see the ghosts, and you are ready to navigate whatever comes over the horizon.

Explanatory notes

What is the impact of the risks on the organisation? What techniques are available to evaluate the impact of such risks?

The Ghost in the Machine: Why Risk Is More Than a Line on a Spreadsheet

We love to think of our organizations as well-oiled machines—a series of gears, levers, and processes humming along in perfect sync. But that's a fantasy. A company isn't a machine; it's a living, breathing organism. It has a heart (its people), a brain (its strategy), and a reputation that acts as its face to the world. And like any living thing, it can get hurt.

A risk isn't just a bump in the road; it's a tremor that can crack the foundation. It's not a singular event but a stone dropped in a still pond, sending ripples outward, touching every part of the whole in ways we might not expect. Understanding these echoes, these ghosts in the machine, is the first step toward true resilience.

The Open Wound: The Bleeding Balance Sheet and the Broken Workflow

When a risk materializes, the first thing we notice is the blood—the gushing red ink on the balance sheet. This is the tangible injury, the kind you can point to. A supply chain snaps, and suddenly, production grinds to a halt, sales targets become fantasies, and you're hemorrhaging cash. A cyberattack isn't just a tech headache; it's a gaping wound of regulatory fines, legal battles, and the colossal expense of rebuilding digital trust from scorched earth.

These are the obvious pains. But then there's the limp. The operational drag. After the initial crisis, the organization isn't running at full speed anymore. Projects are delayed, deadlines are missed, and the frantic energy of "catching up" replaces the smooth rhythm of productivity. Your team is putting in overtime not to innovate, but simply to get back to zero. Imagine a star quarterback playing with a sprained ankle. They're on the field, but they're not the same. That's your organization after a hit—present, but hobbled.

The Phantom Pain: The Scars on Your Reputation and the Derailment of Dreams

The deepest injuries are often the ones you can't see. Long after the financial wound has been stitched up, a phantom pain can linger, haunting the organization for years. This is the damage to your reputation—the most fragile and priceless asset you own.

A food company can survive the cost of a recall, but can it survive millions of customers who now eye their products with suspicion? A tech firm can patch a security flaw, but can it patch the hole in its credibility? In the age of social media, bad news doesn't just travel fast; it metastasizes. It becomes a permanent scar on your public face, a story that's retold with every Google search. Rebuilding that trust is a long, painful, and uncertain pilgrimage.

This reputational damage bleeds into strategy, derailing your brightest dreams. That bold new venture you poured your heart and soul into? It's now on life support because a key partner went under. The forward-thinking, innovative culture you were trying to build is suddenly replaced by a culture of firefighting. Your leadership, once focused on the horizon, is now perpetually looking over its shoulder, mired in crisis management. The organization enters a state of corporate long-COVID—chronically fatigued and unable to reach its full potential.

The Soul of the Organism: The Human Cost

And what about the cells of this organism—the people? A risk event isn't an abstract threat to them. It's a seismic shock to their world. A major safety incident doesn't just create paperwork; it creates trauma. A round of layoffs forced by a financial hit doesn't just cut costs; it shatters morale and seeds insecurity among the survivors.

When people feel the ground beneath them is constantly shifting, they stop planting roots. They live in a state of low-grade anxiety, their creativity stifled by fear. Trust in leadership erodes, replaced by cynicism. The collective spirit—the very soul of your organization—grows weary. Conversely, an organization that faces down risk with honesty, transparency, and a plan shows its people they are valued and protected. It builds a resilient culture not of fear, but of shared courage.

The Doctor's Toolkit: From Diagnosis to Treatment

If your organization is a living thing, then managing risk is a form of medicine. It requires both the art of diagnosis and the precision of science. We need to move beyond simple guesswork and learn to read the vital signs, to understand the patient, and to anticipate what might go wrong.

The Art of Diagnosis: Listening to the Patient (Qualitative Arts)

This is the doctor's bedside manner—the intuitive, experience-driven part of the assessment. It's about understanding the nature of the illness, even if you can't yet measure it in a lab.

The Triage Chart (Risk Matrix): In an emergency room, a doctor doesn't treat patients in the order they arrived; they treat the most critical first. Is it a paper cut or an arterial bleed? A Triage Chart does the same for risks, helping you instantly visualize which threats are life-or-death and which are minor scrapes, so you can focus your energy where it matters most.

The Group Consultation (Brainstorming & Workshops): No single doctor has all the answers. You bring in specialists. By gathering people from every corner of your organization—from the front lines to the executive suite—you get a 360-degree view of the patient's health, uncovering hidden symptoms and potential ailments no single person would have ever spotted.

The Séance with Sages (Delphi Technique): Sometimes, you need wisdom without ego. This technique is like a blind consultation with the world's greatest medical minds. You gather expert opinions anonymously, distill them, and send them back for refinement. This iterative process filters out groupthink and dominant voices, letting the wisest, most objective consensus emerge from the silence.

Playing out the Fever Dream (Scenario Analysis): What if the patient develops multiple complications at once? This technique is about embracing the "worst-case scenario." You write the story of a nightmare—a supply chain collapse and a PR disaster and a market crash. By walking through this fever dream, you expose hidden vulnerabilities and start building a contingency plan for a future you hope never comes.

The Science of the Lab: Reading the Vitals (Quantitative Sciences)

Intuition is vital, but you also need hard data. You need the lab results, the X-rays, and the MRI scans to see exactly what's happening beneath the surface.

Calculating the Price of Pain (Expected Monetary Value): This is where you put a number on the "what if." If there's a 10% chance of an event that would cost you $1 million, the "price of that pain" is $100,000. It's a stark, simple calculation that translates abstract fear into a concrete financial figure, making it impossible to ignore.

Mapping the Pathways of Choice (Decision Tree Analysis): This is a visual map of the future. Every branch is a choice, every leaf an outcome. By plotting out your decisions and their potential consequences—factoring in probabilities and costs—you can clearly see the path that leads to the best possible health, navigating the complex interplay of treatment options.

Finding the Nerve Endings (Sensitivity Analysis): Where is the patient most sensitive? Does a small change in diet (material cost) cause a massive reaction, or is it a change in atmosphere (interest rates)? This analysis pokes and prods your financial model to see which variables cause the biggest swings, showing you exactly where your critical nerve endings are.

The Digital Stress Test (Monte Carlo Simulation): Before clearing an athlete to play, you put them through a stress test. A Monte Carlo simulation is a digital stress test for your business. It runs thousands of different future scenarios at once, throwing random variables at your project to create a distribution of possible outcomes. It doesn't just tell you if you might fail; it tells you the precise probability of it, giving you a deeply nuanced picture of your organization's health under pressure.

Is the Cure Worth the Cost? (Cost-Benefit Analysis): All treatments have side effects and costs. Is the expensive, experimental surgery (a new security system) worth it to prevent a potential illness (a data breach)? This timeless question forces a rational evaluation, ensuring the cure isn't worse than the disease.

From Diagnosis to Resilience: The Path to Corporate Wellness

Ultimately, the goal is not to create an immortal organization, one shielded from every possible harm. That's impossible. The goal is to cultivate a healthy, resilient one. An organization that understands its vulnerabilities, that can diagnose its ailments, and that has the strength and flexibility to heal and adapt.

By embracing this holistic view—seeing our companies not as cold machines but as complex, living systems—we can move beyond mere survival. We can learn to manage the ripples, heal the wounds, and build an organization that doesn't just endure the future, but thrives in it.

Discuss ways of managing risks

The Uncharted Journey: A Guide to Mastering Enterprise Risk

Business isn't a straight line; it's a grand voyage across a vast and unpredictable ocean. Your strategic goals are the distant, sun-kissed shores you aim for. But between here and there lie hidden reefs, sudden squalls, and the siren call of opportunities that might lead you astray. Enterprise Risk Management (ERM) is the ancient and essential art of seamanship for the modern world. It's not about avoiding the ocean; it's about building a vessel so strong, and training a crew so skilled, that you can confidently sail into the heart of the storm and harness its power. This guide is your almanac and your star chart, designed to help you navigate the beautiful, turbulent waters of enterprise.

a. Who's on the Bridge? Manning the Ship of Enterprise

On a well-run ship, every hand has a role in ensuring a safe passage. Risk is not a burden to be shouldered by one person, but a current to be navigated by all. While the captain gives the orders, it is the collective vigilance of the entire crew that sees the ship through the storm.

The Ship Owners (The Board of Directors): From their perch high above the fray, the owners don't steer the ship day-to-day. Their duty is grander: they chart the ultimate destination. They commission the vessel, approve the voyage plan, and hold the Captain accountable for reaching the destination safely and profitably. They are the keepers of the charter, ensuring the entire expedition serves its long-term purpose.

The Captain & Officers (Senior Management): The C-Suite translates the destination on the map into the thrum of the engine and the turn of the rudder. The CEO, as Captain, holds command of the vessel, while the CFO minds the provisions and budget, and the COO ensures the engines run smoothly and the rigging is sound. They foster a culture of vigilance, making sure every officer understands that navigating risk is part of steering toward opportunity. They are the ones with their hands on the wheel.

The Master Navigator (Chief Risk Officer): In the heart of the ship is the chart room, where the CRO lives and breathes. Surrounded by maps of known hazards, celestial charts of market forces, and the latest weather reports, the Navigator's job is not to eliminate storms but to understand them. They are the master of the compass, the sextant, and the barometer, constantly advising the Captain on the safest and swiftest course. They orchestrate the symphony of lookouts and listeners, ensuring a single, clear picture of the journey ahead.

The Lookouts & Deckhands (Risk Management Team): These are the seasoned sailors who spend their days with salt on their faces. They are in the crow's nest, scanning the horizon for signs of trouble. They are on deck, checking the lines, testing the lifeboats, and running the drills. They gather the raw intelligence—the changing color of the water, the speed of the wind—and translate it into practical warnings and preparations for the rest of the crew.

Watch Leaders (Business Unit Managers): Every section of the ship has its leader. These managers are closest to the action—they know the specific groans and creaks of their own department. They are the first line of defense, responsible for the integrity of their part of the hull and the readiness of their crew, ensuring the Captain's orders are followed when the waves begin to rise.

The Crew (All Employees): Ultimately, a ship is only as strong as its crew. Every sailor who ties a knot correctly, every engineer who follows a safety protocol, every cook who prevents a fire in the galley, is managing risk. A ship-wide culture of awareness means that every person, in every role, feels the pitch and yaw of the vessel and understands their part in keeping it afloat.

b. Charting the Course: How Far Do We Dare to Sail?

Before you ever leave port, you must ask three fundamental questions. They sound similar, but they define the very soul of your voyage.

Risk Capacity: The Seaworthiness of Your Ship. This is the most brutal, physical reality. It's the absolute limit of what your vessel can take. How high can the waves get before the hull splinters? How long can you sail without resupply before the crew starves? Risk capacity is not a choice; it is a physical constraint. It is the breaking point beyond which lies catastrophe.

Risk Appetite: The Chosen Destination. This is the soul of the adventurer. It is the conscious, bold decision about which waters you intend to sail. Are you content with the calm, predictable coastal trade routes, earning a modest but steady living? Or do you have an appetite for the legendary riches rumored to exist across the storm-tossed open ocean? A tech startup might aim for uncharted waters, accepting the high chance of being lost at sea for the glory of discovering a new world. This is the strategic "yes" or "no" to a grand adventure.

Risk Tolerance: The Captain's Standing Orders. While appetite is the destination, tolerance is the set of rules for the journey. It's the captain's practical wisdom. "We will venture into the stormy seas (appetite), but if the winds exceed 60 knots, we reef the sails (tolerance)." Or, "We will accept some damage to the rigging, but if any single wave washes over the main deck, we immediately change course." Tolerance provides the guardrails, the specific, measurable limits that keep the crew from recklessly chasing their appetite over the edge of their capacity.

In short, Capacity is what your ship can survive. Appetite is the voyage you choose. Tolerance is how you behave during the voyage.

c. The Shipwright's Blueprints & The Navigator's Almanacs

You wouldn't build a ship without a blueprint, or sail without a chart. Frameworks provide the time-tested structures and principles for your journey.

COSO ERM: The Shipbuilder's Master Blueprint. COSO is the holistic design for a modern, world-class vessel. It integrates every aspect of the ship's existence into a single, cohesive plan. It ensures the ship's command structure (Governance & Culture) is sound, that the voyage's purpose is clear (Strategy & Objective-Setting), that the engines and sails work powerfully (Performance), that the ship is constantly being maintained (Review & Revision), and that the Captain can communicate with the entire crew (Information & Communication). COSO isn't just about avoiding reefs; it's about building a ship designed for speed, resilience, and purpose.

ISO 31000: The Universal Mariner's Guide. If COSO is a specific blueprint, ISO 31000 is the timeless wisdom of the sea itself. It offers a set of universal principles for good seamanship that apply to any vessel, from a canoe to an aircraft carrier. It's a flexible philosophy that emphasizes tailoring your approach to your specific ship and journey (Customized), involving the whole crew (Inclusive), and constantly learning from every voyage (Continual Improvement). It provides a common language for all sailors, everywhere.

Other specialized charts exist for the most dangerous waters, from the Basel Accords for navigating treacherous financial straits to the NIST Cybersecurity Framework for fending off modern-day pirates. The key is to choose the charts that map the waters you intend to sail.

d. Reading the Wind and the Stars: The Science of Seamanship

An ancient mariner could read the sky; a modern navigator uses satellite data. Risk analytics is the science that turns the whispers of the ocean into actionable intelligence, moving you from reacting to the weather to predicting it.

Casting a Wide Net (Data Collection): The foundation is gathering information from every possible source. This means listening to the creaks of your own hull (internal operational data) while also watching the flight of distant birds and the color of the sunset (external market indicators). A holistic view requires weaving all this disparate information into a single, rich tapestry.

Modeling the Storm (Quantitative Assessment): This is where intuition meets mathematics. You can run Monte Carlo simulations to model thousands of potential weather patterns, giving you a realistic range of possible futures. You can use Value at Risk (VaR) to know the single largest wave that is likely to hit you overnight, allowing you to prepare. And you can conduct stress tests by asking, "What if we sailed directly into a hurricane? Would we survive?"

Predicting the Weather (Predictive Analytics): This is the ultimate goal: to see the storm before it forms. By using machine learning to analyze the subtle patterns in the waves and wind, you can forecast dangers like rogue waves (fraud) or sudden doldrums (market shifts) with astonishing accuracy. It's the difference between being a victim of the weather and a master of meteorology.

The Barometer and the Gulls (KRIs): Key Risk Indicators are your early warning system. They are the small, tell-tale signs—the barometer suddenly dropping, the sea birds flying inland—that signal an approaching storm long before you see the clouds. Monitoring these indicators allows you to act, not react.

The Captain's Dashboard (Reporting and Visualization): All the data in the world is useless if the Captain can't understand it at a glance. The art of analytics is to translate complex atmospheric data into a simple, clear dashboard: a heat map showing storm fronts, a compass showing your heading, and a dial showing your speed. This turns raw data into confident command.

Conclusion: The Courage to Sail

In the end, Enterprise Risk Management is not a philosophy of fear. It is not about building an indestructible fortress on land and never setting sail. It is about fostering a deep respect for the power and unpredictability of the ocean. It is about building a vessel and training a crew so exquisitely prepared, so deeply aware, and so powerfully equipped with knowledge that they have the courage to leave the safety of the harbor. It is about seeing the turbulence not as a threat, but as the very wind that can fill your sails and propel you toward a world of discovery and untold value. A great enterprise doesn't just survive the journey; it is built for it.

Role of board and others in the organisation for identifying and managing risks

The Living Organization: A Symphony of Risk and Resilience

Imagine your organization isn't a machine of gears and levers, but a living, breathing being. It has a mind, a nervous system, and countless cells working in concert. In this body, risk isn't just a threat to be neutralized; it's the very energy of life—the force that pushes it to grow, adapt, and thrive. But how does this body navigate a world of both danger and opportunity? It relies on a beautiful, intricate collaboration between its every part.

The Board of Directors: The Conscious Mind

At the very core of this being sits the Board of Directors, the conscious mind. It doesn't worry about the trillions of individual cells; it ponders the big questions of identity and purpose. The board's first job is to define the organization's personality. Is it a cautious soul, preferring well-trodden paths? Or is it a bold adventurer, willing to scale treacherous peaks for the breathtaking view at the top? This decision—its appetite for risk—becomes the organization's guiding philosophy, its internal compass for every journey it undertakes.

This mind is also the architect of the body's essential systems. It doesn't connect the neurons itself, but it approves the master blueprint for the entire nervous system—the Enterprise Risk Management (ERM) framework. It ensures this network connects every limb and organ, so a pain in the foot is felt in the brain, not ignored until it's too late. The board gazes at the strategic map and asks profound questions: "Does our ambition to sprint match the strength of our legs? Are we dreaming of flight when we should be perfecting our stride?" They are the guardians of the body's long-term health, ensuring that its ambitions don't outstrip its capabilities.

To keep a close watch, the mind delegates. An Audit Committee acts like the brainstem, tirelessly monitoring the body's automatic functions—its financial breathing and regulatory heartbeat. A dedicated Risk Committee acts as the prefrontal cortex, scanning the horizon for complex threats and game-changing opportunities, running simulations of the future. Through this elegant structure, the mind stays connected, fostering a culture of self-awareness and encouraging even the smallest cell to signal when something feels wrong.

Management: The Central Nervous System

If the board is the mind, management is the central nervous system, translating intention into action with lightning speed. They are the network of nerves that carry the brain's strategic vision to every muscle fiber of the company. The CEO and senior leaders are the main nerve trunks, and their commitment is the strength of the electrical signal. If their belief in managing risk is weak, the signal fizzles out; if it's strong, the entire body is energized and coordinated.

Management's role is to take the abstract concept of "be adventurous, but not reckless" and turn it into practical reflexes. They are the body's diagnosticians, identifying everything that could cause harm or create strength—from a potential financial infection to an operational muscle strain to a reputational allergic reaction.

When a risk is spotted, the nervous system instantly chooses a response:

Avoid: Pulling its hand away from a burning flame.

Mitigate: Building muscle to protect a weak joint.

Share: Wearing a helmet to transfer the force of an impact.

Accept: Feeling the burn of a tough workout, knowing the pain leads to growth.

A Chief Risk Officer acts as a specialized ganglion, a nerve cluster dedicated to reflexes and sensory integration, ensuring all parts of the nervous system are communicating. But every manager is a vital nerve pathway, responsible for the health and readiness of their own limb or organ. They constantly send status reports back to the brain, letting it know how the body is feeling and responding to the world.

Employees: The Senses, Muscles, and Immune System

And what of the employees? They are everything else. They are the eyes and ears, the nerve endings that feel the texture of the ground and the temperature of the air. They are the hands that build, the legs that move, and the voice that speaks. They are the living embodiment of the organization's culture.

Every employee is a cell in this vast organism. Most are muscle cells, carrying out the daily work with an innate understanding of their function. But they are also the immune system's white blood cells. They are on the front lines, uniquely positioned to spot an invading virus—a flawed process, a compliance breach, a disgruntled customer—long before it shows up on a high-level scan. In a healthy body, these cells are empowered to flag an invader without fear, knowing the entire system will respond to protect itself.

They contribute to the body's resilience not by writing reports, but by living their purpose:

Following the body's rules: Adhering to the safe practices that prevent injury.

Signaling pain: Reporting when something feels wrong or out of place.

Flexing and adapting: Using their on-the-ground knowledge to find better, safer ways to move.

Knowing the emergency plan: Understanding their role when a crisis hits, just as cells know how to clot a wound.

When the mind, nervous system, and every last cell work in this fluid, intuitive harmony, the organization becomes more than a company. It becomes a truly resilient life form—aware, responsive, and ready not just to survive the risks it faces, but to harness them as the very fuel for its extraordinary journey.

Risk mitigation including TARA – transfer, avoid, reduce, accept

The Navigator's Compass: A Human Guide to the Tides of Risk

Forget "Enterprise Risk" as a line item on a spreadsheet. Erase the image of a sterile flowchart. Let's talk about the real thing: the knot in your stomach when a major client goes silent, the shadow of a new competitor on the horizon, the low hum of anxiety about the future you can't quite name. Risk isn't a monster hiding in the dark. It's the weather. It's the unpredictable current, the shifting wind, the sudden squall. You can't command the sea to be still. But you can learn to be a master navigator.

This is where we find the soul of risk mitigation. It's not about building an impenetrable fortress on dry land; it's about building a seaworthy vessel and training a resilient crew. The ancient mariners had their tools, and so do we. One of the most intuitive is a simple compass of four cardinal points: Transfer, Avoid, Reduce, and Accept (TARA). This isn't a rigid set of rules. It's a way of thinking, a conversation with uncertainty.

Transfer: Sharing the Watch

Imagine you're on a long voyage. You are the captain, yes, but you cannot steer, work the sails, and watch for shoals all at once, 24 hours a day. To "Transfer" risk is to have the wisdom to hand the spyglass to someone with sharper eyes for a particular danger. It's about finding a trusted partner to share the watch.

This is more than just buying an insurance policy—though that is the classic example. When you insure your ship, you aren't pretending a rogue wave can't strike. You are entering into a pact that if it does, another will share the burden of rebuilding. Think bigger. When you partner with a cybersecurity firm, you're not just outsourcing a task. You're bringing a seasoned marine onboard whose entire life has been spent studying the patterns of modern-day pirates. You are admitting, "Your expertise in this specific area exceeds my own, and my crew is better served focusing on our destination." Transfer is an act of strategic kinship, not of offloading a problem, but of building a stronger alliance against it.

Avoid: Reading the Skies, Choosing Your Course

The wisest captain is not always the one who sails headfirst into the hurricane. Often, it's the one who reads the ominous stillness in the air, studies the flight of the gulls, and makes the call to stay in a safe harbor until the storm passes. To "Avoid" a risk is the ultimate act of foresight. It's the profound wisdom to say, "No. That particular sea is not for us."

This is the hardest choice, because it often means turning your back on a siren's song of opportunity. It's choosing not to launch a product in a market where the political currents are too treacherous. It's deciding against using a revolutionary but volatile material in your manufacturing because the potential harm to your people and your world is a price you refuse to pay. Avoidance isn't cowardice; it's courage. It is the deep, quiet confidence to choose your own course, knowing that the greatest victories are sometimes the battles you wisely choose not to fight.

Reduce: Mending the Sails, Reinforcing the Hull

This is the daily rhythm of life on the ship. It is the constant, diligent work that separates a weathered vessel from a wreck. To "Reduce" risk is to engage in the endless act of preparation. It's the crew tightening the rigging, patching the sails, and running drills until their response to a crisis is pure muscle memory.

Every time you train an employee on a new safety protocol, you are reinforcing the hull. Every time you diversify your supply chain, you are adding a backup rudder. Every firewall you erect, every layer of security you add, is another lookout in the crow's nest, scanning the horizon for threats. Reduction isn't a single, grand gesture. It's a culture of vigilance. It's the thousand small, deliberate acts of craftsmanship and care that build a deep, unshakable resilience into the very timbers of your organization. It's how you prepare the ship to not just survive the storm, but to sail through it with strength.

Accept: Embracing the Sea

No matter how skilled the navigator or how sturdy the ship, the ocean will always be the ocean. There will be chop. There will be swells. There will be days of unnerving fog. To "Accept" risk is to find peace with this fundamental truth. It is the captain's understanding of their vessel's strength—knowing it can handle the routine tossing of the waves without needing to fight every single one.

This isn't recklessness; it's earned confidence. You accept the minor software glitch that isn't worth dismantling your entire system to fix. You accept the slight market fluctuations because you've built a financial reserve—a deep keel—to keep you stable. Acceptance requires a profound self-awareness. It asks, "What is our appetite for the sea? How much roll and sway can we tolerate and still hold our course?" It is a calculated embrace of reality, a decision to conserve your energy for the waves that truly matter.

The Captain's Hand on the Tiller

In the end, this compass—TARA—is just a tool. Its true power comes from the human hand that holds it. Risk mitigation is a story we tell ourselves, a culture we build, and a conversation we have every single day. It requires leaders who listen to the faintest whispers of concern from their crew and a crew that feels safe enough to voice them.

The goal isn't to find a mythical, placid lake where no risks exist. The goal is to become such masterful sailors, with such a well-tended ship and a well-drilled crew, that you have the confidence to navigate any waters. It's about transforming fear of the unknown into a deep and abiding respect for it, allowing you to guide your enterprise through the labyrinth of what-ifs with not just resilience, but with grace.

Assurance mapping, Risk register

Charting the Unknown: Your Ship, the Storm, and the Art of Staying Afloat

Running a company is a bit like captaining a ship on a vast, unpredictable ocean. You have a destination in mind—growth, innovation, success—but between you and that distant shore lie hidden reefs, sudden squalls, and the occasional sea monster. Enterprise Risk Management, stripped of its corporate jargon, is simply the ancient art of seamanship. It's about knowing your vessel, reading the weather, and trusting your crew to navigate the dangers.

And in the modern captain's toolkit, two instruments are more vital than any other: the ship's log, where every potential danger is charted, and the watch system, which ensures that vigilant eyes are always on the horizon. These are the risk register and assurance mapping, and they are the keys to not just surviving the voyage, but mastering it.

The Risk Register: Your Ship's Log and Nautical Charts

Forget spreadsheets and dusty binders. Imagine your risk register as a living, breathing set of nautical charts laid out on the captain's table. It's not a list of fears; it's a map of reality, marked with warnings, wisdom, and a clear course of action. Every notation on this chart is a story waiting to be told.

"Here Be Dragons" (The Risk Description): We don't just write "cybersecurity threat." We describe the beast. Is it a swift pirate raid aiming to steal our cargo of data? Or is it a mythical kraken from the deep, a system-wide failure that could pull the whole ship under? We give the danger a face and a name.

The Officer of the Watch (The Owner): Every charted danger has a designated officer responsible for it. When the barometer drops, who is on deck? When a strange shape appears on the horizon, whose eyes are trusted to be watching? Accountability isn't a buzzword; it's knowing who to wake up when the storm hits.

Reading the Weather and Gauging the Waves (Likelihood & Impact): How dark are the clouds? Are the waves mere chop, or are they towering walls of water that could crash over the deck? We combine these readings into a Storm Warning Level. A "Category 5" risk—a likely event with catastrophic consequences—demands all hands on deck, now.

The Ship's Defenses (Existing Controls): What keeps us afloat right now? It's the reinforced hull, the well-drilled sailors, the watertight compartments. These are our current defenses—the fire drills, the backup navigation systems, the strong locks on the cargo hold.

Plotting a Safer Course (Further Action): The sea is always changing, and so must our strategy. The charts tell us what more we must do. Do we need to teach the crew a new knot, reinforce the rigging, or build a taller crow's nest for a better view? This transforms our map of dangers into a clear plan for the voyage ahead.

The Churn We Accept (Target Residual Risk): No captain can promise a perfectly calm sea. After we've prepared, trained, and reinforced, there's a level of swell and spray we accept as part of the journey. This is the calculated risk we're willing to live with to reach our destination.

This living chart turns abstract anxieties into concrete landmarks. It's the foundation of confident navigation, allowing us to steer with purpose, not just react to the waves.

Assurance Mapping: A Watch System You Can Trust

So, you have your charts. You know where the dangers lie. But how do you know your lookouts are actually looking? How can you be sure your instruments are calibrated and your crew is ready? That is the role of assurance mapping—your ship's watch system.

It's a plan that ensures every critical part of your ship and every patch of ocean is being watched by a reliable set of eyes. These eyes belong to your assurance providers, your trusted lookouts.

The Crew on Deck (First Line of Defense): These are the sailors handling the sails, swabbing the decks, and manning the helm. They live and breathe the ship's daily operations. They are the first to feel the shift in the wind or hear the groan of a strained mast. Their diligence is the first and most vital layer of safety.

The Ship's Officers (Second Line of Defense): This is your First Mate, your Navigator, your Boatswain. They don't steer the ship moment-to-moment, but they oversee the crew, design the emergency drills, check the navigation calculations, and ensure ship-wide protocols are followed. They make sure the crew is ready for the storm before it arrives.

The Captain's Walk (Third Line of Defense): This is internal audit. The Captain, stepping away from the charts, takes a personal, independent tour of the entire vessel. They check the bilge pumps, inspect the emergency rations, and quiz the crew, providing an objective assessment of the ship's true readiness, challenging assumptions and uncovering hidden weaknesses.

The Seasoned Harbor Pilot (External Assurance): Sometimes, you need an outside perspective. You bring aboard a seasoned local pilot to navigate a treacherous channel, or a master shipwright to inspect the hull in drydock. These experts bring knowledge of dangers your own crew might never have seen, offering unbiased, critical insight.

Assurance mapping is the art of layering these watches. It's how you:

Find the Blind Spots: It immediately reveals if everyone is staring at the storm clouds on the port bow while a pirate ship is silently approaching from the stern.

Avoid a Crowded Crow's Nest: It prevents you from posting three of your best lookouts to watch the same, calm patch of water, which is not just inefficient but dangerous.

Post Your Best Eyes on the Foggiest Horizon: By understanding the whole system, you can assign your most trusted resources to watch over your greatest vulnerabilities.

Inspire a Sound Night's Sleep: For everyone from the newest passenger to the ship's owners, this integrated system provides profound confidence that the vessel is in capable hands.

Sailing Through the Storm, Together

Imagine the charted risk is "A Pirate Raid on the Ship's Manifest (Customer Data)."

Your charts (risk register) would mark the threat, assign the Master-at-Arms as the owner, and note your defenses: the guards, the locked captain's cabin. You'd plot a safer course: installing a stronger door.

Your watch system (assurance map) then confirms these defenses work. The crew (IT team) patrols the digital decks. The officers (Security department) design the patrol routes. The captain's walk (internal audit) runs a surprise drill to test the guards' readiness. And finally, you bring in a harbor pilot (an external cybersecurity firm) who knows the pirates' latest tactics to test your defenses.

Together, these two tools transform risk management from a corporate exercise into a human story of foresight, diligence, and trust. They allow an organization to be more than just a vessel tossed about by the whims of the market.

They allow it to become a well-captained ship, with a clear map of the seas, a vigilant crew at the ready, and the resilience to sail confidently toward any horizon, no matter what storms may lie ahead.

Risk reports and responses and Ethical dilemmas associated with risk management

Every business has a heartbeat. It's the rhythmic pulse of production, the hum of collaboration, the silent, steady flow of capital. But alongside this vibrant lifeblood, there are whispers. They are the ghosts of what could go wrong: the market that might turn, the technology that could fail, the customer's trust that might break. To pretend these whispers don't exist is to invite disaster. To listen to them, to understand their language, is the art of risk management.

Think of a risk report not as a spreadsheet of doom, but as the company's central nervous system. It's the network that feels the chill of a coming storm, the faint tremor of an unstable market, or the sharp pain of a security breach. For this system to work, it can't scream in a language of static and jargon. It must speak plainly, telling a story the entire organization can understand. A great report doesn't just list monsters in the dark; it draws a map. It shows where the biggest dragons lie sleeping, what treasures they guard, and which ones are beginning to stir. It illuminates the path, pointing out the cracks in the armor and suggesting how to forge a stronger shield, giving the mind of the enterprise—its leadership—the clarity it needs to act, not just react.

And what a deliberate dance that action is. Once the whispers are understood, the organization must choose its steps. Sometimes, the wisest move is avoidance—to see a chasm ahead and decide to chart a new course entirely, even if it means leaving a potential prize behind. Other times, it's about reduction; staying the course but building stronger walls, reinforcing the bridge, or learning to quiet the storm's fury. Then there is transfer, the savvy of hiring a champion to fight a battle for you, most often through the shield of insurance. And finally, there is acceptance, the bravest step of all: to look at a risk, understand its power, and decide to walk into the storm with open eyes, believing the potential reward is worth the journey.

This is where the map ends and the moral compass begins. The path is almost never clear, and it's in these murky crossroads that an organization's true character is forged. What happens when the numbers on a page demand one thing, but the safety of a human being demands another? A company discovers a flaw in its most popular product. To speak of it is to invite financial ruin and public scorn. To stay silent is to let a potential poison seep into the world, endangering the very people who keep the business alive. This isn't a business decision; it's a moment the company's soul is weighed.

Or consider the burden of knowledge. A leader sees a brutal economic winter on the horizon, one that could freeze the pensions of the employees who have given their lives to the company. When does a leader's duty to prevent panic outweigh their duty to tell the hard truth? How do you guard the flame of hope without lying about the coming darkness? There is no easy formula here, only the delicate, painful balance of stewardship and transparency.

These dilemmas echo in every choice. Do you spend millions fortifying your digital walls against unseen hackers, or do you use that money to build a new community center? It becomes a question of family: do you reinforce the roof or put more food on the table tonight? The temptation to present a flawless face to the world is immense. It's easy to paint over the cracks, to sing a cheerful tune while the hull takes on water, a practice that doesn't just hide risk, but betrays trust.

Ultimately, managing risk is less a science of prediction and more a practice of wisdom. It's the recognition that the whispers of what could go wrong are not there to frighten us, but to guide us. Responding to them with courage, with honesty, and with a profound respect for people—customers, employees, and the wider community—is what separates a business that merely survives from one that builds a lasting legacy. It is the art of not just navigating the shadows, but of strengthening the light.

Explanatory notes

How is risk managed in the organisation? How is responsibility for various aspects of risk management distributed in the organisation? How does the organisation align its risk tolerance, appetite and capacity to its decisions and actions? What risk management frameworks are there? How is risk information communicated to the organisation?

A Conversation with the Future

Here, we don't think of risk management as a set of rules or a department in the basement. We see it as a living, breathing conversation with the future. It's a way of listening for the whispers of what might be—both the promising opportunities and the cautionary tales—so we can navigate the journey ahead with wisdom and courage. It's a shared story, a collective instinct we cultivate every day, woven into the very fabric of who we are and what we aim to achieve.

Listening for Whispers

The conversation begins with listening. Deeply. We press our ear to the ground of our own operations, but we also gaze out the window at the horizon. We're listening for the faintest signals: the rumblings of a market shift, the static of a new cyber threat, the shadow of a coming regulation, or even the subtle change in a customer's tone. This isn't a job for a select few. We ask everyone to be a scout, to keep their senses sharp and share what they notice. Every employee, from the front desk to the executive suite, is an essential voice in this first part of the dialogue.

Understanding the Stakes

Once we hear a whisper, we have to ask: How loud could it get? And what would it say if it shouted? This is where we try to understand the nature of a potential risk. Sometimes, this is a storytelling session, a creative exercise in "what if?" where we map out complex scenarios with our best minds. Other times, we bring out the scales and rulers, using quantitative analysis to measure the potential fallout in real numbers. This process isn't about creating fear; it's about gaining clarity. It allows us to build a map of maybes, focusing our energy not on every shadow, but on the ones that could truly alter our path.

Writing Our Reply

After listening and understanding, we must respond. Our reply to a potential risk isn't always the same; it's a carefully considered choice.

Sometimes, the wisest reply is to walk a different path (Avoid). If a new trail looks beautiful but is prone to landslides, we might choose another route to the summit.

More often, we choose to shore up our defenses (Reduce). We bolster the walls, upgrade our digital locks, and practice our fire drills. This is about making ourselves stronger and more resilient in the face of a challenge we know we must meet.

In some cases, we ask a friend to hold some of the weight (Transfer). This is the essence of insurance—partnering with someone who can help us bear a burden that would be too heavy to carry alone.

And finally, there are times we look a risk in the eye, understand its nature, and choose to live with it (Accept). Not all storms require us to run for cover. For some, we simply put on a good coat and carry on, accepting the rain as part of the journey.

An Unending Dialogue

This conversation isn't a solo; it's an orchestra, and responsibility is the sheet music everyone shares.

Our Board of Directors and senior leaders are the conductors. They don't play every instrument, but they set the tempo and the key—our overall appetite for risk. They champion the music and make sure every player feels its importance.

A dedicated Enterprise Risk Management team acts as the composers and arrangers. They study the great works of risk management—frameworks like COSO or ISO 31000—and adapt them into a score our organization can play beautifully. They provide the tools and guidance that allow everyone to perform in harmony.

But the music itself comes from the players—our people on the front lines. Our departmental managers and their teams are the virtuosos. The IT specialist hears a discordant note in the code; the finance expert spots a flaw in the ledger; the operations manager sees a potential snag in the supply chain. They manage the risks in their own sections, playing their part with skill and awareness.

Finally, our internal audit team is our most discerning critic. After the performance, they give us honest feedback, telling us where we were in tune and where we might need more practice, ensuring our conversation with the future remains honest and effective.

This entire process is guided by a clear understanding of our limits. We know our risk capacity (the absolute maximum storm we can weather), our risk appetite (the kinds of challenging expeditions we're excited to take on), and our risk tolerance (how much of a detour we're willing to accept on any given project). Every major decision is a note in this grand composition, checked to ensure it harmonizes with the whole piece.

By treating risk not as a threat to be silenced but as a dialogue to be engaged in, we build more than just resilience. We build a culture of shared awareness, turning uncertainty from an obstacle into an invitation to become smarter, stronger, and more prepared for the beautiful and complex future we are striving to create.

Area B: Strategic Risk

Analyse risk associated with formulating strategy

The Navigator's Chart and the Unruly Sea

Every great venture, whether it's a corner coffee shop or a global tech giant, is a ship setting sail for a distant shore. And every leader is a captain, holding a chart. This chart is the strategy. We trust it. We pour over its lines and markings. But we often forget that this chart is drawn not with ink, but with belief. It's a tapestry of guesses, hopes, and assumptions about the world—a world that refuses to sit still. If that ghostly ink proves false, the ship, no matter how sturdy, is sailing blind.

The Ghostly Ink: Reading Between the Lines of Our Beliefs

Look closer at your own strategic chart. What silent whispers is it built upon?

First, there's the 'X' that marks the spot—our assumption about the treasure island, the market. We sketch it with bold lines, believing we know its size, its climate, its growth. We assume the natives—our customers—will greet us with open arms, eager for what we have to offer. But what if the island is shrinking? What if the inhabitants' tastes have changed, and they no longer value our particular brand of gold, preferring simpler, more authentic treasures instead? A strategy built on a mythical island is a voyage to nowhere.

Then, we mark the positions of other vessels—our assumptions about the competition. We label them as slow-moving merchant ships, predictable in their routes. This was Blockbuster's fatal error; they saw a fleet of similar galleons and never imagined a new kind of vessel, a submersible named Netflix, that could travel unseen beneath the waves and surface in every harbor at once. They assumed the battle would be fought with cannons, not by changing the very nature of the sea.

Next, consider the stars we navigate by—our assumptions about technology. A shipping company might assume that bigger sails and stronger hulls are the future. They chart their course by the predictable power of the wind. But what if, over the horizon, a rival is quietly installing a steam engine? A force that makes the wind irrelevant? To mistake a technological revolution for just another gust of wind is to be left in the doldrums, watching the future speed away.

The chart is also filled with notes on the law of the sea—assumptions about the political and regulatory tides. We count on open trade routes, favorable treaties, and the benevolence of distant kings. A green energy vessel sails confidently, powered by the winds of government subsidy. But politics is a fickle god. A new monarch can declare a trade route closed overnight, leaving the most well-planned expedition stranded in hostile waters.

And finally, the most dangerous assumption of all is the one we make about our own ship and crew—our internal capabilities. The captain proudly believes his vessel is sound, his crew loyal, his rations plentiful. But is it true? Is there a hidden rot in the timbers? A simmering mutiny in the galley? An ambitious plan to round the Horn might assume a seasoned, fearless crew, only to discover it's staffed by sailors who have never seen a storm.

This ghostly ink isn't the problem. Belief is necessary. The danger lies in mistaking it for fact—in treating the chart as the ocean itself. The wisest captains are the ones who are constantly looking up from the paper, tasting the salt in the air, and asking, "What if the map is wrong?"

When the Sea Rises: Navigating the Storms of Disruption

Even the most accurate chart is useless when the sea itself decides to rewrite the rules. These are the disruptions—the rogue waves and sudden whirlpools that can splinter timber and send the most confident navigator spiraling off course.

The most visible of these is the rogue wave of technology. It doesn't just rock the boat; it's a towering wall of water that changes the ocean's very surface. The internet didn't just make retail ships faster; it allowed anyone to build a port in their own home. Generative AI isn't just a new kind of sextant; it's a magical force that can conjure new maps out of thin air, forcing every artist, writer, and coder to question what it means to create.

Then there are the shifting tides of the market. These are slower, more powerful currents driven by the pull of a new moon. A generation that values the memory of a journey over the ownership of a jeweled chest changes the destination for everyone. A growing desire for goods that don't poison the waters creates a powerful current toward sustainability, pulling unprepared ships onto the rocks of irrelevance.

Sudden, violent economic squalls can rise without warning. A financial hurricane (a recession) can snap the mast and tear the sails to ribbons. An unexpected fog of inflation makes every piece of rope and every barrel of rum ruinously expensive. The recent chaos in the world's supply chains was a global storm that showed just how fragile the network of shipping lanes truly is.

The map can also be redrawn by distant kings and queens. A new law, a new tax, a new war—these are the decrees that can turn a safe harbor into a blockaded port overnight. Suddenly, your trusted route is forbidden territory, forcing a terrifying, impromptu detour through uncharted waters teeming with sea monsters.

Finally, the very stars we navigate by can shift their alignment. These are the deep social and cultural changes. The constellations of what we value—fairness, inclusion, well-being, purpose—are rearranging themselves in the night sky. A captain who continues to navigate by the old, familiar stars of hierarchy and hustle will find themselves hopelessly lost, unable to attract a crew or find a welcoming port, because the world itself is now oriented toward a different true north.

The goal, then, is not to build an unsinkable ship or to possess a perfect, unchanging map. That is a fool's errand. The true art of strategy is to build a resilient vessel and cultivate a weather-wise crew. It is to foster a culture that loves the telescope more than the chart, that has the courage to tack against a familiar wind, and that knows the difference between a destination and a direction. The journey is not a straight line drawn on brittle paper; it is a living, breathing dance with an unpredictable and wondrous sea.

Analysis of strategic choice, Scenario planning

Of Captains and Currents: Navigating the Fog of Business

Every leader is a captain of a ship. The organization is your vessel, your team is your crew, and your objective is a distant, promising shore. But the sea between here and there is not a placid lake; it's a vast, unpredictable ocean of commerce, churning with hidden currents, rival vessels, and the ever-present threat of a sudden squall. To simply point your ship toward the horizon and hope for the best is not strategy; it's a gamble.

True navigation requires more than a compass and a dream. It requires the wisdom to choose your course wisely and the foresight to imagine the weather you haven't yet seen. This is the art of strategic choice, illuminated by the lighthouse of scenario planning.

Choosing Your Voyage: The Soul of Strategy

At its heart, a strategic choice is the act of charting your course. It's the profound decision of not just where you're going, but how you intend to get there. This isn't about minor adjustments to the rigging; it's about deciding whether you're a nimble trading schooner, a formidable battleship, or a luxury liner promising an unparalleled experience.

This choice is a conversation between two things: your ship and the sea.

First, you must know your ship. What is its nature? Is its hull built for speed or for strength? This is your organization's internal reality—its unique talents, its secret recipes, its battle-tested technologies, and yes, its creaky planks and leaky sections that need tending. Ignoring the state of your own vessel is the fastest way to sink.

Second, you must read the sea and the sky. What are the prevailing winds of the market? Where are the powerful currents of technological change heading? Who are the other ships in these waters, and what are their intentions? Are there regulatory storms brewing on the horizon? A captain who doesn't respect the ocean is a captain who will be humbled by it.

The Ghosts of "What If?": Risk and the Unseen Reef

Every voyage is haunted by the ghosts of "what-if." What if our navigation is wrong? What if pirates—or disruptive competitors—appear over the horizon? What if the promised land is a barren rock? This is risk, the silent passenger on every strategic journey.

To pretend it isn't there is to sail blindfolded. This is why a modern ship has sonar and radar—the tools of enterprise risk management (ERM). But these tools aren't just for avoiding disaster. They are for understanding the depths beneath you. Integrating risk into your strategic choice means you're not just looking at the map; you're actively scanning for the unseen reefs and monstrous deeps that could scuttle your entire enterprise. It turns fear of the unknown into a healthy respect for it, making your chosen course not just ambitious, but intelligent.

Telling Tales of the Future: The Magic of Scenario Planning

No sailor can predict the weather with perfect certainty a month from now. But a wise sailor tells stories. They tell tales of a sudden, violent squall. They whisper legends of a season of miraculous, favorable winds. They prophesize the discovery of a new, bountiful trade route.

This is the essence of scenario planning. It is not fortune-telling; it is the disciplined craft of storytelling about the future.

You begin by asking: What are the two or three great, unknowable forces that will define our journey? The direction of the wind? The temper of the sea? These are your key uncertainties.

Then, you weave them into different tales, different plausible futures.

The "Brave New World" Scenario: A story where technological currents are swift and favorable, opening up new channels of trade for those bold enough to navigate them.

The "Perfect Storm" Scenario: A grim tale where regulatory hurricanes and competitive battleships make passage treacherous and costly.

The "Shifting Tides" Scenario: A narrative where customer tastes change like the tide, stranding ships that were built for a world that no longer exists.

By living in these stories for a while, you ask: How would our ship, on its current course, fare in each of these tales? Where are we vulnerable? Where might we find an unexpected advantage?

Building the All-Weather Ship: The Grand Integration

Here is where the magic happens. You take your chosen course—your strategic choice—and you hold it up to the light of your imagined futures.

Scenario planning becomes your ultimate stress test. You can see if your strategy, which looks so brilliant in the calm harbor of today, is brittle enough to snap in the first gale of your "Perfect Storm" scenario. If it is, it's not a robust strategy.

This integrated approach forces you to build an all-weather ship. You still choose a primary direction, but you build in flexibility. Perhaps you add reinforced sails for heavy winds, or extra cargo space to capitalize on a sudden opportunity. You develop contingency plans—the seafaring equivalent of emergency drills—so that when the unexpected happens, your crew doesn't panic. They adapt.

This fusion of strategic choice and scenario planning creates a profound shift. You move from making a single, high-stakes bet on one forecast to developing a posture of perpetual readiness. You build an organization that is not just efficient, but resilient; not just focused, but aware.

The Endless Horizon

In the final analysis, leadership isn't about having a perfect, unerring map. Such a thing has never existed. It's about becoming a master mariner. It's about knowing your vessel intimately, respecting the awesome power of the sea, and having the wisdom to prepare for futures you can't yet see.

By weaving strategic choice and scenario planning together, you are doing more than just managing risk. You are fostering a culture of resilience and foresight. You are preparing your crew not just to survive the storms, but to sail confidently toward any horizon, ready to discover the new worlds that await. You are preparing for tomorrow, today.

Stress-testing strategy

The Shakedown Cruise: Why Your Business Needs to Sail into a Perfect Storm

Every enterprise, at its core, is a vessel sailing on an ocean of uncertainty. Some days the waters are calm, the heading is true, and the destination seems inevitable. But on the horizon, storms are always gathering. These aren't your average squalls; they are the perfect storms of economic collapse, digital piracy, and geopolitical chaos.

So, how do you know if your ship is truly seaworthy? You don't wait for the hurricane to find out. You run a shakedown cruise. You deliberately steer it into a simulated tempest. This is the soul of stress testing. It's not a dry, academic exercise for the compliance department. It's the corporate equivalent of a flight simulator, designed to let you experience a catastrophic failure in a place where you can walk away, learn, and rebuild stronger. For the modern CGMA professional, this isn't just risk management; it's the art of strategic foresight.

Writing Your Corporate Horror Story (So It Never Comes True)

Traditional risk assessments are like checking the gauges on your ship—valuable, but limited. They tell you about individual parts in isolation. Stress testing is different. It's about finding out what happens when the engine fails, a rogue wave hits the deck, and the navigator's charts are suddenly written in a foreign language all at the same time.

It uncovers the hidden chain reactions, the terrifying domino effects that single-point checks will always miss. To do this, you must become a master storyteller of plausible disasters.

This process begins not with spreadsheets, but with imagination.

Define the Fear: First, ask the most fundamental question: What are we truly afraid of? Is it a liquidity crisis where the financial well runs dry? A catastrophic loss of reputation that makes you a pariah? A capital crunch that forces you to shutter operations? Naming the nightmare is the first step to conquering it.

Author the Scenarios: Now, build the world around that fear. Don't borrow generic plotlines. Your scenarios must be bespoke thrillers tailored to your industry and location.

An economic scenario isn't just 'X% drop in GDP.' It's 'Our top three clients go bankrupt, consumer spending on non-essentials evaporates, and the cost of raw materials doubles.' Make it visceral.

A technology scenario isn't just a 'cyberattack.' It's 'A ransomware attack locks every critical file two days before our quarterly earnings report is due.'

Then there's the truly creative part: Reverse Stress Testing. Instead of asking what happens if a storm hits, you ask: What kind of monster storm would it take to sink us completely? This forces you to confront the "black swan" events, the unthinkable scenarios you'd otherwise dismiss.

Fueling the Simulator and Reading the Wreckage

A simulation is only as good as the world it creates. That world is built on data—clean, comprehensive, and ruthlessly honest data. 'Garbage in, garbage out' isn't strong enough. In stress testing, it's 'Garbage in, a false sense of security that leads to total disaster out.' Your financial history, market intelligence, and operational metrics are the fuel for this engine.

Once you run the simulation, the real work begins. The results will come back looking like the wreckage of your company. Don't just stare at the carnage. Become an investigator. Why did this division buckle while another held firm? What flawed assumption, what hidden dependency, acted as the fatal flaw? The numbers are the symptoms; your job is to diagnose the underlying disease.

Forging Armor from Insight

Here lies the entire purpose of the exercise. A stress test that ends in a filed report is a monumental waste of time. Its true value is in turning harrowing foresight into immediate action.

The analysis provides a blueprint for resilience. It's a literal to-do list for survival.

If your revenue is dangerously concentrated, it's time to diversify.

If your operational supply chain snapped under pressure, it's time to build redundancy.

If your capital reserves evaporated, it's time to reinforce your financial shock absorbers.

This is how you forge armor. You identify the weakest points revealed in the simulation and you reinforce them with smarter strategies, stronger capital, and more robust contingency plans.

The Captain's Briefing

Finally, these findings cannot live in the shadows. They must be communicated with stark clarity to the leadership team, the board, and any relevant stakeholders. This isn't about presenting complex models. It's about telling a clear story: "We sailed the ship through a simulated hurricane. The port-side engine failed, and we took on water here, and here. This is our plan to reinforce the hull and rebuild the engine."

Ultimately, a robust stress-testing strategy is a declaration that you choose to be the author of your company's fate, not a victim of circumstance. It is an ongoing commitment to rehearsing for disaster, not to live in fear, but to ensure that when the real storm inevitably comes, you have the skill, the strength, and the confidence to sail right through it. For a CGMA, this is how you build an enterprise that doesn't just endure the future, but thrives in it.

Explanatory notes

What are the risks that the strategy of the organisation is wrong? What are the sources of such risks? How does the organisation evolve its strategy in a dynamic environment to keep it relevant?

The Navigator's Folly: Why a Bad Map Sinks the Ship

Every organization fancies itself a sturdy vessel on a grand voyage. The strategy is its map, its compass, its North Star—the sacred document promising a journey to lands of profit and renown. But what happens when the map is a fantasy? What happens when the navigator is steering by a star that isn't there?

The ship doesn't just miss its destination. It founders. It becomes a ghost ship, a cautionary tale whispered in boardrooms and classrooms—a monument to a flawed journey. For those who study the art of navigating these treacherous corporate seas, like professionals pursuing the CGMA designation, learning to spot a bad map isn't just a skill. It's the key to survival.

The Sound of a Ship Taking on Water

When the strategy is wrong, the first sign isn't a single, catastrophic crack in the hull. It's a series of slow, insidious leaks, each one threatening to pull the entire enterprise under.

It begins with the sound of gold coins slipping through the floorboards and into the deep. This is the financial drain—the treasure chest of capital and resources poured into building a new dock on a deserted island, or hunting a mythical beast. The investment vanishes into the abyss, leaving the ship lighter on treasure but heavier with the water of debt and distress.

Then comes the quiet dread of being left behind. While your vessel chases a mirage, other ships, with better maps, discover new worlds teeming with opportunity. You sail past emerging continents of technology and shifting archipelagos of customer desire, oblivious. This is the competitive disadvantage, a slow drift into irrelevance, where your ship becomes a relic in a world that has charted a new course.

On deck, chaos reigns. This is operational turmoil. The crew, once unified, now rows in different directions. Sailors painstakingly polish brass that should be jettisoned, while others try to patch holes with canvas meant for the sails.

No one understands the captain's orders because the orders themselves are nonsense. People work furiously, sweating and straining, but their effort is a whirlwind of motion that moves the ship nowhere.

Soon, the ship earns a reputation. It's known in every port not for its glorious arrivals, but for its constant, aimless wandering. This is the poison of reputational damage. Trust, that invisible wind in the sails, dies. Customers stop waiting at the docks. The best talent refuses to sign on. Rebuilding a name is like trying to recapture the wind in a bottle.

Finally, you feel the soul of the ship begin to die. The crew, the heart of the vessel, gives up. They see the map is flawed and the destination is a lie. Why row toward a storm? Why give your all for a voyage to nowhere? This is the great talent exodus. The most skilled sailors, the ones who can read the real stars, quietly lower the lifeboats in the dead of night and row toward steadier ships, leaving behind a skeleton crew to go down with the vessel.

The Ghosts in the Charting Room

A bad map is never drawn by accident. It is born from a confluence of human folly and willful blindness.

Sometimes, it's simply hubris in the charting room. The navigators—the leadership—rely on old, faded maps from a different era. They sketch coastlines from memory and wishful thinking, without sending out scouts to see what the world actually looks like. They might even have a good map, but if the captain can't rally the crew to follow it, the ink is wasted.

Other times, a dangerous harmony takes hold. It is the curse of groupthink, an echo chamber where every officer agrees that sailing directly into the hurricane is a brilliant maneuver. Dissenting voices are treated as mutiny. A single, flawed idea gains unstoppable momentum because no one has the courage to stand up and shout, "There be dragons!"

Then there's the danger of a navigator who never looks out the window. This is a failure to scan the environment. The sea of commerce is a living thing, with shifting tides, sudden squalls, and new currents of technology and culture. A captain who only looks at their map, and not at the waves crashing over the bow, is navigating toward yesterday. They are the Blockbuster captain, assuring the crew that those tiny Netflix speedboats pose no threat.

Even when the navigator sees the iceberg ahead, the ship itself may be too stubborn to turn. This is organizational inertia. A rigid structure, a culture that punishes mistakes, a bureaucracy tangled like old fishing nets—all these can render a vessel un-steerable. The command to turn the rudder is given, but the rudder is rusted in place.

And perhaps most fundamentally, a map can be wrong because it was drawn in the dark. A lack of real data is like navigating by folklore instead of by compass. When intuition replaces information, every decision is a gamble. You are essentially asking the sea to be what you feel it should be, not what it is.

Learning to Read the Living Sea

In a world of constant change, the very idea of a fixed, permanent map is the most dangerous fantasy of all. The sea is alive. A successful organization must therefore become a living ship, one that evolves with the water it sails upon.

This begins by turning the entire ship into a sensory organ. Constant environmental scanning is more than a lookout in the crow's nest; it's every sailor feeling the wind shift, tasting the salt in the air, and listening to the songs of distant shores. It is an unending process of gathering intelligence—through data, through conversation, through intuition—to build a dynamic, ever-changing picture of the world.

Next is to build a vessel that can dance on the waves. A culture of agility means the ship can tack and jibe in an instant. It means empowering every crew member to spot a risk or an opportunity and act without waiting for a formal command from the captain's quarters. It's about celebrating the scout who returns with news of failure, for that knowledge is just as valuable as finding treasure.

The strategy, then, is not a sacred parchment locked in a chest. It is a living chart, constantly being redrawn. The five-year plan is dead. In its place are shorter voyages, quarterly explorations, and the use of scenario planning—charting courses for multiple possible futures, so that no storm ever comes as a complete surprise.

This living chart must be drawn with the ink of integrated risk management. Understanding risk isn't about avoiding storms; it's about knowing precisely how much wind your sails can take. It's about measuring the depth of the water before you weigh anchor. Risk intelligence is the ballast that keeps the ship stable, allowing it to take calculated chances without capsizing.

And through it all, there must be the captain's voice. Clear, steady, and honest. Leadership is the art of telling the story of the voyage, explaining why the course is shifting, and assuring every single person on board that their work, their oar in the water, is critical to reaching the ever-shifting horizon.

Ultimately, a truly great organization isn't one with a perfect, unchanging map. It's a living, breathing vessel, with a crew and a captain who are masters of the sea. They understand that the journey itself is the destination, and they have the courage, the wisdom, and the agility to sail confidently toward whatever lies beyond the edge of the map.

Evaluate the sources and impact of reputational risks

Sources of reputational risk, Impact of reputational risk on strategy

A company has a body—its assets, its buildings, its people. It has a mind—its strategy, its patents, its data. But it also has a soul. And that soul is its reputation. It's invisible, yet it's the most valuable thing a company owns. It's the silent hum of trust in a customer's mind, the quiet confidence of an investor, the spark of pride in an employee's heart. It's a story, told in a thousand small actions over years. But stories can be rewritten in an instant, and a beautiful tale can become a cautionary one overnight.

The threats to this soul, this reputation, don't always arrive like a thunderstorm. Sometimes, they are more like a sickness—starting from within or catching a chill from the world outside.

The Rot from Within

Often, the most dangerous threats are born right at home, in the heart of the organization itself.

Imagine a master chef renowned for their craft. If they start serving spoiled food, the magic is gone. This is the risk of a broken promise. When a company's product or service—its core offering to the world—fails, it's not just a defect; it's a betrayal of the trust that was placed in them.

Then there's the poison in the soil: unethical behavior. This is the executive who dips into the company coffers, the sales team that lies to close a deal, the culture that values profit over people. It seeps into the foundations of the company, and when the public gets a glimpse of that moral decay, they don't just see a mistake; they see a character flaw. They question the very heart of the organization.

In our world of glass houses, a cracked digital vault is a devastating blow. We hand over our most personal data, believing it will be guarded. When that trust is shattered by a data breach, it's a profound violation. We feel exposed and foolish for believing the promises of safety. The company is no longer seen as a guardian, but as a careless host of a party where everyone got robbed.

And what about the people who make the magic happen? If a company is a family, then a toxic home life will eventually spill out onto the front lawn for all to see. Exploited workers, a culture of fear, a lack of respect—these stories don't stay behind closed doors anymore. They travel on whispers and social media posts, painting a picture of a company that is ugly on the inside. The best people leave, and the best customers follow.

The Storms from Without

Sometimes, the threat gathers on the horizon, coming from the world the company operates in.

A single story can become a wildfire. The media, with its insatiable appetite for drama, can take a spark of truth (or even a flicker of falsehood) and fan it into an inferno. In the 24/7 echo chamber of news and social media, a narrative is chosen, and the company becomes the villain in a global play. The trial happens on Twitter, and the verdict is delivered in retweets.

This digital mob can form in minutes. A single customer complaint, a misunderstood ad, a clumsy executive quote—it can go viral, gathering outrage like a snowball rolling downhill. This isn't a reasoned debate; it's a sudden, overwhelming wave of public emotion that can crash over a company before it even understands what's happening.

Then there are the watchful eyes over the garden wall. Activist groups and watchdogs exist to hold power to account. They might expose environmental damage, unfair labor practices, or harmful products. Their campaigns are designed to be loud and uncomfortable, shining a spotlight on practices the company would rather keep in the shadows.

Even a neighbor's success can cast a shadow. When a competitor shines brighter—by innovating faster, behaving more ethically, or connecting more deeply with customers—it can make you look dull and outdated by comparison. Their light reveals your darkness.

Finally, the climate itself can change. The values of society are not static. What was acceptable a decade ago might be abhorrent today. A company that clings to old ways of thinking about the environment, social justice, or corporate responsibility will find itself out in the cold, seen as a dinosaur in a world that has moved on.

When the Soul is Wounded

A damaged reputation isn't just a PR problem; it's a strategic catastrophe that sends shockwaves through the entire organization.

The first tremor is felt in the wallet. Customers walk away. Investors get spooked. The stock price, which is just a number representing collective belief, tumbles. The flow of money, the lifeblood of the company, slows to a trickle.

Next, the heart of the company begins to weaken. The most talented people—the innovators, the leaders, the dreamers—don't want to be associated with a tainted name. They quietly update their resumes and head for the door. The company starts to suffer a brain drain, leaving it less capable of healing itself.

Then come the official visitors. Regulators and lawyers are drawn to scandal like sharks to blood. Suddenly, the company is buried in audits, investigations, and lawsuits. Energy that should be spent on creating and building is spent on defending and explaining.

Growth becomes a dream deferred. Trying to expand into new markets with a damaged reputation is like trying to make friends after being accused of a terrible crime. Doors are closed. Partnerships evaporate. The world becomes a smaller, more hostile place.

And in the end, it all comes down to one thing: trust. Trust is the invisible thread that connects a company to everyone it touches. When that thread is cut, everything falls apart. Marketing becomes noise. New products are met with suspicion. Apologies ring hollow.

A company can spend all its time focused on growth, but if it doesn't tend to its soul, it's building a beautiful house on a foundation of sand. Protecting that good name, that story, that hum of trust, isn't a defensive tactic. It is the central act of ensuring survival. It is the soil from which all success, or all failure, grows.

Risks of unethical behaviour and Impact on brand and reputation of organization

Think of a company not as a logo or a stock ticker, but as a living, breathing organism. It has a heart—its people. It has a voice—its brand. And it has a soul—its integrity. But when unethical choices are made, a sickness takes root. It doesn't announce itself with a thunderclap; it begins as a silent infection in the marrow, a moral decay that, if left unchecked, will ravage the entire body.

This sickness first poisons the lifeblood: the customers. Imagine you've been betrayed by a trusted friend. That's what it feels like for a customer who discovers the product they believed in was a lie, or the service they relied on was built on deceit. It's not a simple business transaction anymore; it's a personal wound. They don't just switch brands; they recoil. They warn their friends. That trust, once shattered, calcifies into a scar. You can apologize, you can promise to change, but they will always touch that scar and remember the pain you caused.

Inside the organization, the infection spreads to its very soul—the employees. Working in a place that has lost its moral compass is like living with a constant, low-grade fever. The energy vanishes. The passion sours into cynicism. People no longer walk in with purpose; they drag their feet, their best ideas locked away for an employer who deserves them. The most talented, the ones with the strongest moral character, are the first to leave. They are the healthy cells fleeing a diseased body. What's left behind is a culture of apathy and distrust, where whispering in the hallways replaces collaborating in the boardroom. Whistleblowers emerge, not as traitors, but as the body's last, desperate attempt to expel the poison.

Then, the body begins to bleed. The financial wounds opened by unethical behavior are not clean cuts; they are gaping, hemorrhaging gashes. Regulatory fines aren't just costs; they are punishments that drain the company of its strength. Lawsuits become a chronic condition, a constant drain on energy, money, and focus. Leaders who should be charting a course for the future are instead trapped in endless depositions, trying to suture wounds from the past. The company's stock price—its public pulse—flatlines, as investors flee the scent of sickness. The very capital needed for healing and growth is lost, bleeding out onto the pavement of public record.

But the most devastating toll is on the company's face to the world: its reputation. A brand is a story, a promise. When that promise is broken, the story becomes a tragedy. The company is no longer known for its innovation or its quality, but for its scandal. The name becomes a shortcut for greed, deception, or harm. Every news report, every social media hashtag, is like a fresh blow to a bruised face, a constant, public reminder of its disgrace. Trying to recruit top talent is like asking someone to move into a condemned house. Forging new partnerships is like trying to find a dance partner when everyone knows you have the plague.

This isn't just a storm that passes. It's a change in the climate. Competitors with strong ethical cores suddenly look like safe harbors, attracting the customers and talent you've abandoned. The company becomes isolated, defined not by its potential, but by its pathology.

For those who are the stewards of an enterprise's health, like a CGMA professional, the lesson is clear. You are not just an accountant; you are a physician. Your job is not merely to count the company's money, but to check its vitals, to safeguard its soul. The cure for this sickness isn't found in a crisis management plan; it's found in prevention. It's in building a powerful immune system—a culture so deeply rooted in integrity that the infection of unethical behavior can never find a place to grow. It's about ensuring the organization is not just profitable, but whole. Because in the end, a reputation is the one asset that, once it dies, can never be brought back to life.

Explanatory notes

What is reputational risk and why is it an important strategic risk? What are the types and sources of reputational risks and what is their impact on the organisation? How can they be managed?

Your Company's Reputation is Made of Glass

Imagine the company you've built—or the one you work for—isn't a fortress of brick and steel. Imagine it's a house made entirely of glass. Every decision, every product, every interaction is visible for the world to see. For years, you've polished this glass, making it gleam with trust and integrity. It's your most beautiful, most valuable asset.

This glass house is your reputation. And reputational risk is the terrifying realization that a single, carelessly thrown stone can shatter the whole structure. It's not a storm cloud on the horizon; it's a hairline crack that suddenly appears right beside you, threatening to splinter into a thousand pieces before you can even react. It's the loss of the one thing that money can't easily buy back: belief.

Why a Single Crack Can Bring Down the House

A risk, like a financial loss or a product delay, is a problem to be solved. But a reputational hit is different. It's not just a problem; it's a catalyst that makes every other problem a hundred times worse.

Think of that hairline crack. A financial scandal isn't just about the money that vanished; it's the crack that appears in the glass. Suddenly, customers peer through it with suspicion. Investors, seeing the fracture, get nervous about the integrity of the whole structure. That single crack, caused by one issue, spreads under the pressure of public opinion, weakening everything.

In a world woven together by clicks and shares, that crack doesn't spread slowly. It travels at the speed of a viral tweet. A story, true or false, can circle the globe while you're still in a meeting trying to figure out what happened. Your gleaming glass house can become a web of fractures in a single afternoon. You spent decades polishing the glass. It can be shattered in minutes.

The Stones That Get Thrown

Where do these devastating blows come from? It's not always a boulder hurled with malicious intent. Often, it's a small, unexpected pebble from a place you never thought to look.

The Clumsy Hand Inside: Sometimes, the damage comes from within. An operational failure—a massive data breach, a faulty product that needs recalling, or an airline whose planes are perpetually delayed. These aren't acts of malice, but they are stones dropped on the glass floor. The public doesn't care if it was an accident; they just see the crack.

The Rot in the Foundation: Other times, the problem is deeper. An ethical breach. The discovery of sweatshop labor in your supply chain, a C-suite executive's history of toxic behavior, or a deliberate "creative" accounting scheme. This is like realizing the very ground your glass house is built on is unstable. When people believe you are fundamentally rotten, the entire structure loses its legitimacy.

The Tremors from the Market: While a missed earnings report is a financial problem, a pattern of poor performance becomes a reputational one. It creates tremors that shake the glass. No one wants to invest their money, their career, or their trust in a house that seems to be perpetually trembling on the verge of collapse.

The Inspector's Hammer: This is the blow from legal or regulatory non-compliance. Ignoring environmental laws, flouting safety regulations, or breaking privacy promises. These aren't just costly fines; they are the official stamp of untrustworthiness. The inspector has come and tapped your wall with a hammer, publicly declaring it unsafe.

The Hailstorm of Whispers: And then there is the modern phenomenon of social media. This isn't one stone; it's a hailstorm of a million tiny pebbles. A viral video of a rude employee. An influencer's angry tweet. A coordinated campaign of negative reviews. Each one is a tiny chip, but together they can leave your glass opaque and battered.

Living in the Wreckage

When the glass shatters, the impact is total.

The cold wind rushes in. Sales drop. Customers, who once felt safe and sheltered by your brand, now feel exposed and betrayed. They take their business elsewhere, to a house that feels more secure.

Investors flee the ruins. Your stock price plummets. Who wants to own a piece of a shattered building? Raising money becomes impossible, and potential partners see you as radioactive.

No one wants to move in. The best talent—the brilliant minds you need to rebuild—will walk right past your wreckage. They'll choose to work in a place that's intact, admired, and secure. Your current talent may start looking for the exits, tired of living amongst the shards.

The area is cordoned off. Regulators, who may have once trusted you, now put you under a microscope. Every move is scrutinized, every form double-checked. You operate under a constant cloud of suspicion.

Rebuilding is a slow, painful process. You can't just sweep up the glass. You have to earn back trust, piece by painful piece. This takes time, humility, and a monumental amount of effort. Some stains on the ground, some memories of the collapse, never truly fade.

How to Reinforce the Glass

You can't stop every stone from being thrown. But you don't have to live in fear. Managing this risk is about making your glass stronger, being ready to act, and building a culture that respects the house it lives in.

Become the Architect. First, you must study your own blueprints. Conduct a fearless assessment. Where are the weakest panes of glass? What are your vulnerabilities? Don't just look at the obvious financial risks; look at your culture, your supply chain, your social media presence. Know where the cracks are most likely to appear.

Install Shatterproof Film. This is mitigation. You strengthen the glass before it gets hit. This means robust cybersecurity, ethical training that people actually believe in, a real and respected code of conduct, and whistle-blower policies that protect, not punish. These are the invisible layers that can turn a shattering blow into a manageable crack.

Have an Emergency Plan. When you hear the sound of cracking glass, you must have a plan. Who speaks? What is the first, honest message you will share? How will you show you're taking it seriously? In a crisis, silence is guilt. Speed, transparency, and genuine empathy are the tools you use to contain the damage.

Create a Culture of Caretakers. The strongest defense is a team where every single person understands they live in the glass house, too. This comes from the top. When leaders act with integrity, it becomes the air everyone breathes. An ethical culture isn't a policy; it's a collective instinct to protect the home.

Listen for the Tapping. Finally, you must be constantly listening. Monitor social media, news, and customer feedback not as a chore, but as a security system. Often, before the stone is thrown, you can hear the faint tapping of discontent. Catching that early whisper allows you to address it before it becomes a deafening roar.

In the end, protecting your reputation is about treasuring your good name as the most fragile and precious thing you own. It's about being the vigilant, dedicated caretaker of your own glass house, ensuring it stands clear and strong for all the world to see.

Explain Governance Risks

The role of board and its committees in managing strategic risk and Failure of governance and its impact on strategy

The Captains, the Crew, and the Kraken in the Deep

Every company is a ship on a vast, unpredictable ocean. Some days the sailing is smooth, the winds are fair, and the destination seems certain. But the sea is always changing. Beneath the sunlit surface, ghost currents shift, phantom reefs materialize, and leviathans of risk—the kind that can splinter a hull and drag a mission to the depths—are always lurking.

In this high-stakes voyage, the board of directors is the command crew on the bridge. Their job isn't to scrub the decks or hoist the sails; it's to chart the course through the heart of the storm. They are the keepers of the map, the watchers of the weather, the ones who must ultimately answer the most fundamental question: What kind of ship are we? Are we a nimble explorer, darting into uncharted coves for rare treasure? Or are we a heavily armored galleon, built to withstand anything the main trade routes can throw at us?

This choice—the company's "risk appetite"—is everything. It's the soul of the strategy. Too timid, and the ship rots in the harbor, falling behind sleeker vessels. Too reckless, and you're chasing legends straight into the kraken's lair. The board's sacred duty is to provide oversight, to stand on the quarterdeck and ask the tough questions, ensuring the captain (management) isn't just staring at the horizon with wishful thinking, but is truly prepared for the monsters and the magic of the deep.

To see the whole ocean, the command crew relies on specialized officers, each with a unique vantage point:

The Chief Engineer & Quartermaster (The Audit Committee): This is the crew that lives in the heart of the ship. They are obsessed with integrity—not just of the numbers in the logbook, but of the vessel itself. They are constantly tapping the hull for weaknesses, checking the soundness of the rigging, and ensuring every system is running as it should. They work with the auditors—the outside inspectors—to make sure no rot has set in below the waterline, guarding against the siren call of cutting corners on compliance and controls.

The Crow's Nest Lookout (The Risk Committee): More companies are realizing they need a dedicated lookout, someone whose only job is to climb to the highest point with a long glass and scan the horizon. This committee isn't focused on the engine room; they're looking for the glint of a pirate sail, the tell-tale sign of a coming squall, or the distant shimmer of a new, undiscovered land of opportunity. They see the big picture, the world outside the ship, and they translate that panoramic view into actionable intelligence for the entire command crew.

The Crew Officers (Other Committees): From the people who manage the crew's morale and pay (Compensation Committee) to those who plot new ventures, every officer has a role in managing risk. A smart board ensures their pay structure doesn't reward the crew for sailing the ship aground in a mad dash for treasure, creating a culture of shared responsibility. When these officers talk to each other, the ship sails as one. When they don't, it's chaos.

Adrift: The Ghost Ship of Failed Governance

But what happens when the bridge goes dark? When the command crew is asleep at the wheel, or worse, arguing amongst themselves while the storm rages? The consequences aren't just ripples; they are a tidal wave that swamps the entire enterprise.

Sailing Blind: When governance fails, the flow of information to the bridge is cut. The compass spins wildly, the charts are written in invisible ink, and the lookout's warnings are lost in the wind. The board, starved of real data, makes decisions based on rumor and fear. They mistake a pod of dolphins for a sea monster or a lighthouse for a ghost light, steering the company toward mirages and away from safe harbors.

The Rot Below Deck: With no one inspecting the ship's integrity, weaknesses fester. Small cracks in the hull of compliance widen. The ropes of internal control fray. Financial misconduct, like barnacles, accumulates unseen, slowing the ship down until one day, a single wave is enough to break it apart. This is the story of Enron and Theranos—ships that looked magnificent from a distance but were hollowed out and rotten from within.

The Flag of a Pariah: A ship earns a reputation. When governance failures lead to scandal and collapse, the ship's flag becomes a warning to others. Investors—the backers of the voyage—flee. Talented sailors refuse to sign on. The company's name, once a symbol of pride, becomes a whispered cautionary tale in the taverns of the market. Shareholder value isn't just lost; it's scuttled.

A Ship at War with Itself: Perhaps the most insidious danger is internal decay. Without clear leadership from the bridge, the crew divides into factions. The navigators fight with the engineers, the deckhands ignore the officers. Everyone blames each other as the ship takes on water. The most brilliant strategy in the world is useless if the crew is working to sink itself.

Ultimately, strong governance isn't about bureaucracy or checking boxes. It's about leadership. It is the steady hand, the watchful eye, and the unified voice on the bridge that allows a ship to not only survive the storm but to harness its power. It's the difference between a vessel lost to the annals of history and one whose legendary voyage becomes a legacy.

Separation of the roles of CEO and chairman and Role of non-executive directors

The Two Captains and the Ship's Sages

Imagine a grand, old ship setting sail on a vast, unpredictable ocean. The journey is the company's future, the destination is success, and the stormy seas are the world of risk. For this ship to not just survive, but to thrive, the structure of its command is everything.

So, who's steering this vessel? For years, we've debated a crucial question: should one person be both the on-deck Captain, shouting orders and managing the crew day-to-day, and the Admiral of the fleet, setting the grand strategy from a faraway map room? Or should these be two different people?

This isn't just boardroom jargon. It's the heart of how a company protects itself and grows.

The Hands on the Wheel vs. The Eyes on the Horizon

Think of the CEO as the Captain. They're on the bridge, hands gripping the wheel, feeling the spray of the ocean on their face. They know the crew by name, they feel the ship's every shudder, and they are obsessed with making headway, navigating the immediate waves and currents. Their focus is powerful, immediate, and absolutely vital. They live and breathe the doing.

Now, think of the Chairman as the Admiral. The Admiral isn't on the bridge of just one ship; they're responsible for the entire fleet. They're in the war room, surrounded by maps of distant lands, weather charts, and intelligence reports. Their job isn't to steer the ship today, but to ensure it's sailing towards the right continent, that it's sound enough for the whole voyage, and that the Captain isn't so focused on speed that they're sailing straight towards a pirate cove or a hurricane.

When one person tries to be both—the CEO-Chairman duality—you have a Captain who is also judging their own navigation. They're drawing the map and then claiming they followed it perfectly. It feels powerful, but it's a lonely and dangerous perch. Who's there to say, "Captain, with all due respect, your map is leading us into the storm, not around it"?

Separating these roles provides a beautiful tension, a healthy balance:

An Honest Mirror: A separate Admiral (Chairman) can look the Captain (CEO) in the eye and give real feedback. They can challenge the course, question the speed, and ask the tough questions, because their job isn't to sail the ship, but to protect its journey.

A Clear Conscience: When roles are split, the Captain isn't deciding their own bonus or evaluating their own epic performance. That conflict of interest vanishes, and trust flows back into the system. Everyone knows the decisions are being made for the good of the voyage, not the glory of the Captain.

A Chorus of Voices: An independent Admiral fosters a culture where everyone on the bridge feels they can speak up. The lookout in the crow's nest isn't afraid to shout "Iceberg!" because they know someone at the top is dedicated to listening. This creates a richer, wiser, and safer command deck.

The real magic happens when the Captain is free to be the best damn Captain they can be, knowing the Admiral has their back and is watching the horizon for threats they're too busy to see.

The Sages in the Cabin: The Power of the Outsider's Eye

But it's not just about the two people at the top. Every great ship carries a few passengers who aren't part of the crew—the Non-Executive Directors (NEDs). These aren't just any passengers; they are wise sages. An old astronomer who knows the stars, a master shipwright who understands the groans of the wood, a veteran diplomat who can read the flags of distant ships.

They don't swab the decks or hoist the sails. They observe. They advise. They question. Their power lies in their independence—their "outsider's eye."

Why are these sages so critical for surviving the storms of risk?

They See the Riptides Everyone Else Misses: Because they aren't caught up in the daily hustle of sailing, NEDs can spot the subtle, dangerous patterns the busy crew might overlook. They are the ones who ask, "I know we're sailing fast, but has anyone noticed the water is changing color? I saw this on a different ocean once, just before a maelstrom." They bring the gift of perspective.

They Carry Maps from Other Worlds: These sages have sailed on other ships, in other seas. One might have been a naval strategist, another a merchant explorer. They bring this wealth of diverse experience into the Captain's cabin. When a new threat appears, they can say, "Ah, I've seen this beast before. Here's how we defeated it then." They are a living library of risk-management strategies.

They are the Voice of the Homeland: The sages ultimately answer to the people who funded the voyage—the shareholders. They are the guardians of the mission's integrity, ensuring the Captain doesn't get so obsessed with a personal quest for a sea monster that they forget the goal was to bring back treasure for the kingdom. They hold the ship accountable to its purpose.

They Act as a Moral Compass: In a crisis—when the storm hits and panic sets in—the sages provide a calm, steadying presence. They remind the Captain of the mission's core values. Their detachment is their strength, allowing them to offer measured counsel when emotions are running high.

Ultimately, a resilient company is like a well-run ship. It needs a brilliant, focused Captain (CEO) at the helm and a wise, far-seeing Admiral (Chairman) charting the course.

And just as importantly, it needs a cabin full of sages (NEDs) who, by not being part of the crew, can offer the wisdom, foresight, and courage to see the ship safely through any storm the world throws at it.

Roles of audit committee, remuneration committee, risk committee and nomination committee and Directors' remuneration

Think of a great company not as a static building, but as a majestic ship on a grand voyage. The board of directors are the senior officers on the bridge, setting the course. But they can't steer, navigate the stars, watch the engine, and scan for icebergs all at once. For that, they rely on specialized crews—the board committees. Each has a unique, vital role in ensuring the ship not only stays afloat but reaches its destination with its cargo, crew, and reputation intact.

The Ship's Specialist Crews: A Look at Board Committees

The Audit Committee: Guardians of the Engine Room

Deep in the heart of the ship, the audit committee serves as the chief engineers. Their world is one of precision, integrity, and truth. They don't just glance at the ship's logs (the financial statements); they live in them, ensuring every entry is a true and fair reflection of the journey. Their hands are on the gauges of the company's financial engine, constantly checking the pressure and listening for the slightest hiss or clank that could signal trouble.

They are the ultimate skeptics, questioning everything. Are the systems designed to prevent a stowaway (fraud) or a critical miscalculation (error) robust enough? They are the ones who manage the relationship with the independent lighthouses (the external auditors) that dot the coastline, ensuring their light is bright, unbiased, and truly helpful for navigation. They also listen to the whispers from below deck, overseeing the whistleblowing systems that allow any crew member to report a problem without fear. When the audit committee does its job well, everyone from the cabin boy to the investors on shore can trust that the ship is sound and the captain's reports are true.

The Remuneration Committee: The Quartermasters of Ambition

This committee tackles one of the most human and delicate tasks on board: deciding how to reward the command crew. They are the cartographers of compensation, drawing the maps that link performance to treasure. Their goal is to create a system of rewards that inspires the captain and officers (the CEO and executives) to sail brilliantly, to seek out new, valuable trade routes, and to bring the ship home laden with success for the owners (the shareholders).

They don't just hand out gold coins. They craft a compelling mix: the steady supply of rations (base salary), the bonus for successfully navigating a treacherous storm (performance bonuses), and, most importantly, a share of all future treasures discovered (stock options). This last part is key; it ensures the officers aren't just thinking about the next port of call, but about the long-term prosperity of the entire fleet. In a world watching through spyglasses, this committee must be transparent, proving that the rewards are earned, not just given, and that they fuel the voyage rather than drain the ship's resources.

The Risk Committee: The Watch from the Crow's Nest

On the most complex vessels sailing through the most unpredictable waters, a specialized lookout is needed. The risk committee climbs to the crow's nest with a powerful telescope, dedicated to scanning the entire horizon. While the audit committee worries about the engine within the ship, the risk committee looks outward for every conceivable threat.

They see it all: the shifting political currents that could close a friendly port, the technological pirates threatening to board the systems, the shadow of a rival ship on the horizon, or the distant shape of an iceberg that could sink the entire enterprise. Their job isn't just to shout "Danger!" It's to help the bridge develop the maneuvers to avoid it. They maintain the ship's "danger ledger," tracking every potential storm, rogue wave, or sea monster, and ensuring the crew has a plan to sail around, through, or away from it. They foster a culture of vigilance, making sure everyone on board has one eye on their task and the other on the horizon.

The Nomination Committee: The Master Shipwrights of Leadership

Who gets to serve on the bridge? Who is ready to take the helm if the captain falls ill? These are the questions for the nomination committee, the architects and talent scouts of the command crew. They are the keepers of the ship's soul, ensuring the leadership team is not just skilled, but wise, diverse, and forward-thinking.

They begin by studying the current team on the bridge. Do we have a master navigator but lack an expert in new propulsion technology? Is our communications officer ready for the challenges of the next decade? They look for gaps in skill, experience, and perspective, and then they scour the world for the best talent to fill them. They are constantly planning for the future, building a line of succession so that the ship never finds itself without a steady hand at the wheel. By carefully selecting and vetting each new officer, they ensure the board is a dynamic, powerful team ready for whatever the next voyage may bring.

The Captain's Share: The Art and Science of Paying Directors

How do you compensate those entrusted with the fate of the ship? Directors' remuneration is the fuel for leadership, a delicate pact between the ship's owners (shareholders) and its command crew. It's a blend of stability, incentive, and shared destiny.

Shareholders, the ultimate owners, get a say. They vote on the philosophy behind the pay, ensuring it aligns with their own interests. The remuneration package itself is a carefully crafted cocktail designed to drive the right behavior.

The Basic Stipend: This is the steady ration, the reliable pay that allows directors to focus on their duties without worrying about their own financial stability.

The Performance Bonus: This is the prize for short-term victories—successfully launching a new product is like discovering a rich, uncharted island. It rewards immediate, tangible success.

The Equity Grant: This is the ultimate alignment. Directors are given a piece of the ship itself through share options. Suddenly, its long-term fate is their long-term fate. A rising stock price, reflecting a successful enterprise, directly enriches them. It transforms them from hired hands into co-owners of the voyage, motivating them to ensure the ship not only weathers storms but becomes stronger and more valuable with every passing year.

Ultimately, the goal is a perfect balance: a reward rich enough to attract the most brilliant captains and navigators in the world, yet fair enough that it inspires confidence and trust from all who have a stake in the journey.

Explanatory notes

What is the role of the board in risk management? How does governance risk occur? How is this role governed by the various corporate governance codes and principles?

The Board as Navigators: Charting a Course Through the Seas of Risk

Imagine an organization not as a building, but as a great ship setting sail on a vast, unpredictable ocean. At the helm, you won't find the board of directors with their hands on the wheel, managing the day-to-day swell. Instead, they are in the navigation room, poring over charts, studying the stars, and setting the ultimate course. Their role is one of profound foresight and strategy, for they are the ultimate guardians of the voyage, and in this critical role, risk management is their North Star. It's not about avoiding storms, but about building a vessel strong enough to withstand them and smart enough to navigate them wisely.

The Art of Navigation: The Board's Pivotal Role

The board's role in risk is one of oversight, of setting the "tone from the top." They are the architects, not the builders; the composers, not the orchestra. Their work is to create the framework within which the crew can operate safely and effectively.

First, they must answer a fundamental question: how much adventure are we up for? This is the organization's risk appetite. It's not a stuffy policy document, but the very soul of the strategy. Are we a nimble explorer seeking new worlds, willing to face turbulent waters for untold rewards? Or are we a steady cargo ship, prioritizing a safe and predictable journey? The board doesn't just set a destination; they decide the nature of the voyage itself. This single decision shapes every choice that follows, from the maps they use to the supplies they carry.

Next, the board ensures the ship is seaworthy. They are responsible for the risk management framework – the very blueprints of the vessel. This isn't just about patching leaks as they appear. It's about designing a hull that can withstand pressure, a communication system that is clear and immediate, and a crew that is trained to spot icebergs on the horizon. They must have confidence that the ship's systems for identifying, assessing, and responding to dangers are not just present, but robust and battle-tested.

Then comes the active watch. The board stands on the quarterdeck, telescopes in hand, exercising active oversight. They receive reports from the crow's nest, but they don't take them at face value. They challenge the lookouts, question the captain's assumptions, and scan the horizon for themselves. "Are we sure that's a friendly port? Are our lifeboats truly ready? Is the crew's morale high?" This is not passive observation; it is a dynamic, challenging dialogue that keeps everyone sharp and accountable.

Beyond the mechanics, the board must cultivate a risk-aware culture. This is the invisible current that guides the ship. It's a shared understanding that every single person on board, from the captain to the cabin boy, has a role in keeping the ship safe. It's an environment where a deckhand feels empowered to shout, "I see something!" without fear of being ignored. When the board champions this, risk management becomes more than a manual; it becomes a shared instinct.

Finally, a ship is nothing without a skilled crew. The board ensures that the risk management function is properly resourced. You can't navigate treacherous waters with a frayed map and a broken compass. The board must invest in the best navigators, the most advanced tools, and continuous training to ensure the team is ready for whatever the ocean throws at them.

The Ghost in the Machine: How Governance Risk Emerges

Governance risk is the ghost in the machine, the unseen flaw in the ship's design that can lead to catastrophe. It's what happens when the very structures meant to provide direction and safety fail. It's a rudder that responds sluggishly, a compass that secretly points south.

This phantom menace often appears as a lack of independent oversight. If the navigation room becomes an echo chamber, where the board and the captain are too close, who is left to offer a dissenting view? Who will point out that the chosen course leads directly into a known reef? Without the fresh air of independent thought, the ship can sail confidently into disaster, blinded by its own consensus.

Another form this ghost takes is an information fog. If the captain only shares good news from the journey, or if the reports from below deck are filtered and sanitized, the board is navigating blind. They are trying to chart a course through a dense fog, unaware of the dangers lurking just out of sight. An informed decision is impossible without an unfiltered view of reality.

Conflicts of interest are like a magnetic force that pulls the ship's compass astray. When personal ambitions or hidden agendas influence the navigators, the ship's true destination is no longer the priority. Decisions are made not for the good of the voyage, but for the benefit of a few, leading the entire vessel into perilous waters.

Sometimes, the danger is simply confusion. If no one is quite sure who is responsible for checking the lifeboats or monitoring the weather, these critical tasks can be overlooked. A lack of clear roles and responsibilities creates gaps in the ship's defenses, leaving it vulnerable to risks that everyone assumed someone else was handling.

Ultimately, the most pervasive governance risk is a decaying culture. If the unwritten rules of the ship suggest that cutting corners is acceptable, or that integrity is secondary to speed, a rot sets in. This erodes trust and encourages behavior that, sooner or later, will put the entire enterprise at risk.

The Navigator's Charts: Guidance from Corporate Governance Codes

Fortunately, boards are not left to navigate these waters alone. Corporate governance codes and principles from around the world act as the collective wisdom of countless voyages, offering a set of charts and best practices for safe passage. While not always law, they are the shared language of sound navigation.

These codes are clear: the board must determine the nature of the voyage by defining the principal risks the company is willing to take. They place the responsibility for setting the risk appetite squarely in the navigation room, recognizing that it is a strategic decision of the highest order.

They also mandate the creation of a sound system of internal control and risk management. The codes insist that the ship's blueprints be not only well-designed but also regularly inspected and improved. This is not a one-time task but a commitment to constant vigilance.

Recognizing the need for specialized expertise, these codes often highlight the role of an audit or risk committee. Think of this as a team of master mariners who can take a closer look at the ship's charts and instruments, providing a detailed and expert assessment to the full board.

Transparency is the lighthouse in the fog. The codes call for boards to disclose their approach to risk, shining a light on the dangers they face and how they are being managed. This builds trust with passengers and shareholders, assuring them that the navigators are competent and candid.

Finally, these charts speak to the composition of the navigation team itself. They call for independence, for voices that are not swayed by the captain's charisma or the pressure of the moment. An independent board is a balanced board, capable of seeing the whole picture and making the tough calls necessary to steer the ship through the storm and into safe harbor.

In the grand story of any organization, the board's engagement with risk is not a footnote; it is the central plot. It is the steady hand that guides the ship, the wisdom that reads the weather, and the courage that makes the difficult choices. By embracing their role as navigators and heeding the wisdom of established principles, they can safeguard the voyage, protect its value, and ensure the ship reaches its intended destination, stronger and more resilient than when it began.

Area C: Internal Controls

Analyse Internal Control Systems

Discuss roles and responsibilities for internal controls and discuss the purpose of internal control

Think of a company not as a machine, but as a living, breathing body. Internal controls are its immune system, its nervous system, and its conscience, all rolled into one. They aren't cold, sterile rules in a binder; they are the ingrained habits, the shared instincts, and the collective wisdom that keep the body healthy, strong, and moving toward its purpose.

So what is this body trying to do? What is the deeper "why" behind these invisible systems?

First, it's about protecting its lifeblood: its assets. This isn't just about locking the cash drawer. It's about guarding the very soul of the company—the brilliant ideas scribbled on a napkin, the unique code that powers its products, the trust it has built with its customers. These are the treasures, and controls are the guardians who ensure they aren't squandered, stolen, or simply lost to carelessness.

Second, it's about telling its story truthfully. The financial reports of a company are its autobiography, written in the universal language of numbers. Internal controls are the commitment to honesty in that storytelling. They ensure the story is free from fiction, exaggeration, or convenient omissions. This truthful narrative allows the company to understand itself, and it allows the world—investors, partners, customers—to believe in it. Without this, the story is just noise, and trust is impossible.

Third, it's about moving with grace and purpose. A body at war with itself, with limbs moving out of sync, is clumsy and inefficient. Controls are the choreography that helps the organization move elegantly. They streamline the rhythm of operations, eliminate wasted motion, and ensure that every part is working in concert. This isn't about robotic rigidity; it's about the fluid efficiency of a world-class athlete, where every action is intentional and powerful.

Finally, it's about walking a principled path. In a world of tempting shortcuts and murky ethics, internal controls are the company's moral compass. They are the quiet voice that asks, "Is this right? Is this who we want to be?" They keep the organization aligned with society's laws and, more importantly, with its own stated values, ensuring its journey is one of integrity.

But an immune system, a nervous system, and a conscience don't belong to one person. They are woven into the very fabric of being. The responsibility for them is a beautifully shared endeavor.

Senior Management are the heart and mind of the body. They set the rhythm and the intention. Their belief in ethical, controlled operations pumps through every corporate artery. They don't just write the rules; they live them. Their commitment sends a clear signal to every cell in the organization: "This is how we live. This is who we are." Their leadership is the foundational spark of the entire system.

The Board of Directors and its Audit Committee are the wise elders or the trusted confidantes. They stand slightly apart, offering perspective and oversight. They listen to the body's heartbeat, question its decisions, and ensure it stays true to its long-term health, not just its short-term impulses. They are the guardians of the soul, holding the mind accountable to the promises it has made.

Management at every level are the tendons and ligaments, connecting the grand vision to the daily movements. A sales manager ensuring deals are made with integrity, a warehouse foreman protecting the inventory, an HR director safeguarding employee data—they are the ones translating intent into action. They are on the ground, coaching the muscles and ensuring the choreography is performed correctly every single day.

Every single employee is a living cell in the body. While they may not have designed the system, they are the system. Their adherence to the "healthy habits"—following a security protocol, flagging a strange transaction, speaking up about a concern—is what gives the body its resilience. A single cell that ignores the rules can be the starting point of disease. A community of vigilant cells creates vibrant health.

The Internal Audit team are the specialized T-cells of the immune system. They are an independent force within, constantly roving, testing, and seeking out anomalies. Their job is not to run the body, but to find weaknesses and alert the brain before a small issue becomes a systemic illness. Their objective, dispassionate analysis is crucial for adaptation and healing.

And the External Auditors? They are the annual check-up with the doctor. They provide a fresh, outside perspective, confirming for the wider world that the body is as healthy as it claims to be. Their validation provides a clean bill of health that builds trust and confidence.

Ultimately, internal control is not a project to be completed, but a culture to be lived. It's a dynamic dance of shared responsibility, a collective commitment to creating an organization that is not only successful, but also sound, trustworthy, and built to last. It is the human art of building an enterprise with a strong constitution and a clear conscience.

Analyse the features of internal control systems

The Ship and Its Ghost Crew: A Voyage Through Internal Controls

Every great enterprise is a vessel on a vast, unpredictable ocean. It has a destination—profit, innovation, service—and it sails through waters teeming with opportunity and fraught with peril. There are sudden squalls of market shifts, the lurking leviathans of cyber-attack, the siren song of risky shortcuts, and the jagged reefs of regulation. What keeps this ship from being dashed against the rocks or lost to the depths? It's not just the captain at the helm. It's a silent, ever-present force: the ghost crew.

This crew is the ship's internal control system. You can't always see them, but their work is everywhere—in the tautness of the ropes, the clean lines of the charts, the readiness of the lifeboats, and the unwavering trust the crew has in their captain. They are not a set of rigid rules in a dusty manual; they are the living, breathing discipline of the voyage, the unseen hands that guide the vessel not just to survive the storm, but to harness its winds and sail on with purpose.

The Soul of the Ship: The Captain's Character

The journey begins not with a map, but with the character of the captain and the culture they instill. This is the control environment—the very soul of the ship. It's the unwritten code that hangs in the salt-laced air. Does the captain lead with unwavering integrity, or do they cut corners when no one is watching? The crew knows. They feel it in the way orders are given, in the fairness of the ration distribution, and in the respect shown to the lowest deckhand.

This soul is built from a few crucial timbers. First, is the crew competent? Has the captain chosen skilled navigators, sturdy riggers, and keen-eyed lookouts, or is the ship manned by inexperienced hands? Second, what is the captain's own philosophy? Are they a gambler, chasing every gust of wind, or a master mariner who respects the power of the sea? Finally, a wise captain answers to a council of seasoned ship-owners (the board of directors and audit committee) who review the charts and question the course, ensuring the voyage is for the benefit of all, not just the captain's glory. On a ship with a strong soul, every sailor knows their duty, and doing the right thing is as natural as breathing.

Charting the Unknown: Reading the Winds and Tides

With a worthy crew, the next task is risk assessment. This is the art of reading the sky, the water, and the ancient maps to see the dangers that lie ahead. It's a constant, vigilant gaze toward the horizon. The destination is clear, but what could sink the ship before it gets there?

The ship's officers gather in the map room. They identify the threats: a rival fleet of pirates (competitors), the whispers of a coming hurricane (economic downturn), the risk of a kraken from the deep (a disruptive new technology), or the possibility of rot in the ship's own hull (internal fraud). They don't just list them; they debate them. How likely is the hurricane? If it hits, will it merely rip a sail, or will it snap the mast? Based on this grim calculus, they choose their course. They may decide to sail far around the storm (avoid the risk), batten down the hatches and sail through (mitigate it), or accept that some waves will break over the bow (accept it). This is not about fear; it's about foresight. It's about turning the unknown into a known challenge.

The Hum of a Well-Run Ship: Control Activities

This is where the ghost crew gets their hands dirty. Control activities are the thousand small, deliberate actions that keep the ship in perfect trim. They are the rhythms and routines that prevent chaos.

A core principle is "two sets of eyes." The man who steers the ship is not the one who charts its course. The cook who orders the provisions is not the one who signs for their delivery. This is segregation of duties, and it ensures that a single mistake—or a single act of greed—cannot go unnoticed.

Every significant action requires a confident signature. The first mate must authorize any change in course. The bosun must approve the use of precious supplies. The ship's log is constantly reconciled against the navigator's chart and the supply master's ledger to catch any discrepancy. The captain performs reviews, climbing the rigging to check the crew's work against their own high standards. And deep in the hull, there are physical locks on the gunpowder and the treasure chest—physical controls that guard what is most valuable. These aren't burdens; they are the smooth, efficient hum of a vessel where everything is in its place and everyone is accountable.

The Lookout's Cry: Information and Communication

A ship is blind and deaf without the constant flow of information and communication. This is the lifeblood of the voyage, the network of speaking tubes, signal flags, and urgent cries that connect every part of the vessel.

The lookout in the crow's nest must be able to shout "Land ho!" and have the captain hear it instantly. The engineer in the engine room must be able to report a strange noise without hesitation. This information flows up, down, and across the decks. The quartermaster's report on dwindling water supplies must reach the captain, just as the captain's new orders must reach every sailor.

But it's not just about signals within the ship. The crew must also listen to the outside world—reports from other vessels about safe harbors, warnings of government blockades, or the shifting demands of the destination port. Communication is a culture. It's creating an environment where the greenest deckhand feels empowered to point out a fraying rope to the first mate, knowing their warning will be welcomed, not dismissed. A well-informed ship is a responsive ship, able to tack and turn with grace and speed.

The Captain's Walk: Constant Vigilance

Finally, a ship's systems are only as good as their upkeep. This is monitoring, the final and perpetual duty of the ghost crew. It's the captain's daily walkabout, an unending process of inspection and improvement.

This vigilance is woven into the fabric of the day. The chief mate continuously monitors the crew's performance. The regular balancing of the ledgers is a form of ongoing monitoring. But sometimes, a deeper look is needed. This is when the ship's owners send an inspector for a separate evaluation (an internal audit), a top-to-bottom review of every plank, sail, and cannon. This inspector is impartial, offering a fresh pair of eyes to spot the rot the crew might have missed.

When a weakness is found—a leaky barrel, a slow-to-respond sailor, a map that proves inaccurate—it is addressed immediately. The leak isn't just plugged; the crew investigates why the barrel failed to prevent it from happening again. This relentless cycle of checking, finding, and fixing ensures the ship doesn't just start the voyage in good condition; it grows stronger, faster, and more resilient with every nautical mile.

So, the next time you see a great organization sailing confidently toward its goals, listen closely. Beneath the noise of its engines and the bustle of its work, you might just hear the quiet, steady work of its ghost crew—the unseen architects of its resilience, the silent guardians of its voyage, ensuring it not only weathers the storm but masters the sea. Thank you.

Role of risk manager as distinct from internal auditor

The Chef and The Critic: A Tale of Two Guardians in the Business Kitchen

Imagine your company is a world-class restaurant. The dining room is humming, the stakes are high, and the ambition is to earn a constellation of Michelin stars. In this bustling, high-pressure kitchen, two figures are essential for success, yet they wield their utensils in entirely different ways. One is the Executive Chef, the other is the feared and respected Food Critic.

This is the story of the Enterprise Risk Manager and the Internal Auditor.

The Executive Chef: Our Enterprise Risk Manager

The Chef is a visionary, a creator, a master of flavor and fire. They don't just cook; they architect the entire dining experience. This is our Enterprise Risk Manager.

Their job begins long before the first customer arrives. They design the menu—this is the company's strategic plan. They decide if this will be a restaurant known for its bold, spicy risks or its classic, comforting reliability. This decision, this "flavor profile," is the organization's risk appetite.

The Chef is on the floor, in the thick of it. They are proactive, forward-looking, and deeply hands-on. They are the first and second lines of defense. They see a shipment of fish that looks a day past its prime—that's a supply chain risk they must immediately mitigate. They hear a buzz about a rare truffle season—that's an opportunity they must seize.

They are constantly tasting the sauces, adjusting the heat, and training their line cooks. "Watch the flame on that pan!" is a lesson in managing operational risk. "This is how we plate our signature dish" is a procedure to ensure quality and protect the brand's reputation. They are embedding a culture of excellence and awareness into every single person in the kitchen, making risk management a shared reflex, not a dusty rulebook.

The Chef's goal is to create a masterpiece, a meal that delights and astounds. They take calculated risks, blending exotic ingredients (new technologies) with timeless techniques (sound business practices) to achieve greatness. They are a partner in creation, their eyes fixed on the future plate.

The Critic: Our Internal Auditor

Now, enter the Critic. They do not work in the kitchen. They have never salted a pot of water in this restaurant. Their power lies in their independence, their objective palate, and their seat in the dining room. This is our Internal Auditor.

The Critic represents the third line of defense. Their role is not to cook, but to provide assurance. They arrive after the meal has been conceived and prepared, looking back on the final product. Their job is to assess, with an unbiased eye, if the Chef's vision translated into a flawless experience.

Their perspective is retrospective and methodical. They ask:

"The menu promised a medium-rare steak. Was it delivered as promised?" This is testing an internal control.

"Was the kitchen sanitary and up to code?" This is auditing for compliance.

"For the price, did the overall experience deliver value?" This is assessing efficiency and effectiveness.

The Critic's review isn't given to the Chef over a friendly beer. It's published for the world to see—or in our case, delivered directly to the restaurant's owners (the Board of Directors' Audit Committee). This independent reporting line is everything. It ensures their judgment is unclouded by the kitchen's internal politics or the Chef's passionate defense of their creations. They are the objective truth-teller, offering a clear, unfiltered assessment of what is actually happening.

A Michelin Star Collaboration

So, are the Chef and the Critic adversaries? Far from it. A brilliant Chef doesn't fear the Critic; they learn from them. The Critic's review—"The soufflé was breathtaking, but the fish was slightly overcooked"—is invaluable feedback. It tells the Chef precisely where the process broke down, helping them strengthen their techniques for the next service.

Likewise, a wise Critic reads the Chef's menu and understands their intent before they ever take a bite. The risk register, curated by our Chef, helps the Critic focus their review on the most ambitious and high-risk dishes.

When the creator and the evaluator work in harmony, sharing insights without compromising their distinct roles, the restaurant thrives. The Chef builds the systems for success, and the Critic independently verifies their integrity. Together, they transform a simple business into a resilient, celebrated institution, capable of weathering any storm and consistently delivering on its promise of greatness. They are the two guardians who ensure the enterprise isn't just a flash in the pan, but a name that stands for enduring excellence.

Control systems in functional areas and Operational features of internal control

Forget the clanking gears of a machine or the abstract notion of an "unseen hand." Think of a business as a living, breathing organism. It has a mind, a heart, a nervous system, and a deep, instinctual drive to survive and thrive. In this biological metaphor, internal controls aren't chains or cages; they are the body's innate intelligence—the subconscious reflexes, the powerful immune system, and the steady rhythm of a healthy heart that keep it alive in a world full of challenges.

Let's explore the anatomy of this corporate creature. Each functional area is a vital organ, and each has its own unique, built-in system for self-preservation.

The Finance department is the circulatory system, and cash is its lifeblood. The goal is to keep this blood flowing cleanly and purposefully, without clots or hemorrhages. A control like requiring two signatures on a check isn't just a rule; it's the heart's sophisticated valve system, ensuring blood only flows where it's supposed to. It prevents the lifeblood from leaking out through fraud (a hemorrhage) or being blocked by a single, malicious actor (a clot). Daily bank reconciliations? That's the body constantly checking its own pulse, instantly sensing if the pressure is off or the rhythm is wrong, allowing it to heal before a small problem becomes a catastrophic failure.

Then you have Operations, the body's muscular system. This is where things are built, created, and moved. It's all about strength, precision, and endurance. A quality control check on an assembly line is the body's muscle memory. It's the practiced, perfect form of a master craftsman, instinctively catching a flaw before it's even fully formed. An inventory system isn't just about counting widgets; it's the body's metabolism. It ensures there's enough energy (raw materials) to power through a workout without bonking, but also that it isn't storing so much excess fat (unsold goods) that it becomes sluggish and unhealthy.

What about Human Resources? This is the organization's central nervous system. It's about communication, sensation, and the well-being of every cell in the body. A background check for a new hire is the body's immune response, identifying a potentially harmful foreign agent before it can enter the system and cause disease. Strict access controls on employee data are the brain protecting its most private thoughts and memories. And a fair performance review system? That's the nervous system ensuring that every part of the body feels valued and is functioning in harmony, preventing the internal pain and turmoil of a disgruntled, rebellious workforce.

Even Marketing has its place in this ecosystem. It's the face and voice of the organism—how it presents itself to the world. Brand guidelines are the body's consistent personality. They ensure that the face the world sees today is the same one it saw yesterday, building trust and recognition. The multi-layered approval process for a new ad campaign is the crucial filter between the brain and the mouth, preventing the organism from saying something foolish or offensive that could cause irreparable harm to its reputation.

These individual organ systems are amazing, but they are all governed by a deeper, holistic intelligence. This is the essence of internal control's operational features, the subconscious programming that allows the entire organism to function as one.

This programming begins with the Control Environment, which is nothing less than the body's conscience or soul. Set by the brain (leadership), it's the inherent ethical character of the organism. Does it act with integrity? Does it value its own health? A strong conscience informs every action, making ethical behavior an instinct, not a chore. A weak one invites disease.

Next comes Risk Assessment, which is simply the body's five senses. The organism is constantly scanning its environment. It feels the heat of a new competitor, sees the storm of a market shift on the horizon, and hears the whispers of new regulations. Internally, it feels the pang of hunger from a weak supply chain. It's a continuous, dynamic process of sensing danger and opportunity, allowing the body to react before it gets hurt.

Those reactions are the Control Activities. These are the body's reflexes. When the senses detect a threat, the body doesn't need to think; it acts. Segregation of duties is the reflex that makes you use two hands to lift something heavy and precious. Authorizations are the conscious permissions the brain gives before the body takes a significant risk. Reconciliations are the body's blink, a constant, quick reset that keeps its vision clear. These are the ingrained, automatic safeguards that protect the organism from moment to moment.

Of course, none of this works without Information and Communication—the full, unimpeded flow of the nervous system. A pain signal from the foot must reach the brain instantly. The brain's command to run must reach the legs without delay. In a business, this means clear reports, open conversations, and a culture where every cell (employee) knows its role and feels safe to report a problem. A breakdown in communication is like a pinched nerve; the organism becomes clumsy, slow, and unable to protect itself.

Finally, there is Monitoring, which is the body's gift of homeostasis and healing. The body is constantly monitoring its own temperature, its blood sugar, its healing wounds. An internal audit isn't a punishment; it's the body sending in white blood cells to a potential infection to assess the damage and begin repairs. This constant self-assessment ensures that small injuries heal and don't fester into chronic, life-threatening conditions.

So, when you think of controls, banish the image of a rigid, bureaucratic machine. Instead, picture a vibrant, resilient living thing. These systems aren't about restriction; they're about health. They are the silent, powerful, and deeply intelligent systems that allow an organization to not just survive, but to adapt, to heal, and to thrive in a complex and ever-changing world.

Explanatory notes

What are the roles of internal control systems in managing risks? What are its key features and why?

Imagine a business isn't a machine, but a world-class symphony orchestra standing on the stage of 2025. The global audience is discerning, the acoustics are unpredictable, and the musical score—the company's strategic plan—is more complex and demanding than ever before. In this concert hall of commerce, what separates a breathtaking performance from a chaotic mess? It isn't just the skill of the musicians or the vision of the conductor. It's the invisible discipline that binds them together: the art of internal control.

This art is a subtle masterpiece of risk management, played in several movements.

First comes the Overture of Prevention. This is the quiet, meticulous work done long before the first note is played. It's the sheet music distributed to each player, clearly marking their part and no one else's. The violinist doesn't play the cello's part; this segregation of duties prevents a single musician from throwing the entire piece off-key through error or ego. It's the conductor tapping the stand, setting the tempo and volume, ensuring no section overpowers another—these are the authorization limits that prevent a rogue tuba from blasting over a delicate flute solo. This opening movement is about designing harmony from the start, ensuring the performance begins with grace and confidence.

Next, we hear the Chorus of Detection. Because even in the most practiced orchestra, a string can snap or a note can be missed. This is where the conductor's keen ear comes in—the detective control. It's the first-chair violinist catching a subtle dissonance from the back row and giving a slight nod to bring them back in tune. It's the regular review of the performance recording—like reconciling a bank statement—to find that one flat note that could signal a deeper issue with an instrument or a player. This movement isn't about blame; it's about listening intently and making real-time adjustments to keep the music pure and the performance on track before a minor slip becomes a major embarrassment.

Beyond these, internal controls compose the Bridge of Strategy. This isn't just about playing the notes correctly; it's about interpreting the music. The controls provide the conductor with the feedback needed to make daring artistic choices. How fast should this passage be? How soft should this crescendo feel? This is the organization deciding its risk appetite. This shared understanding of the music, from the conductor to the last chair in the percussion section, fosters a culture where every player feels responsible for the collective sound. They don't just react to mistakes; they actively feel the music and manage their part within the whole.

Then there is the Cadenza of Compliance. Every great concert hall has rules—fire codes, union laws, public safety standards. The orchestra must honor them. Internal controls are the orchestra's commitment to playing within these rules, whether it's protecting the personal data of their patrons (GDPR) or adhering to fair labor practices. This isn't about fear of the fire marshal; it's about earning the trust of the audience and the community, proving that the orchestra's brilliance is matched by its integrity.

And finally, the Grand Finale of Trust. The performance ends, the lights come up, and the audience—investors, partners, customers—decides whether to applaud. The reliability of financial reporting is that final, resounding chord. It is the proof that the performance was as magnificent as it sounded. Strong controls ensure the recording of the concert is an honest reflection of what was played, free from distortion or artificial enhancement. This integrity builds a legendary reputation, ensuring sold-out halls for years to come.

So, what are the core elements that create this symphony of control?

It all begins with The Conductor's Baton: The Control Environment. This is the soul of the orchestra. It's the passion, ethics, and integrity that flows from the conductor. If the conductor is disciplined, respectful, and dedicated to artistic excellence, that "tone at the top" inspires every musician to give their best. Without this shared belief in the music, the most detailed score is just paper.

Then comes Reading the Score: Risk Assessment. A great conductor doesn't just read the notes; they study the score for its dangers and its dreams. They identify the treacherous passages, the complex rhythms, the potential for discord, and where the true beauty lies. This is the art of understanding what could go wrong—from a sudden tempo change to a complex harmonic shift—so you can focus the orchestra's practice on the parts that matter most.

These are followed by The Art of Playing in Concert: Control Activities. These are the tangible actions, the specific techniques of bowing, breathing, and striking that bring the music to life. It's the physical lock on the case of a multi-million dollar Stradivarius violin. It's the rule that the person who writes the music isn't the one who collects the ticket revenue. These are the practical, hands-on habits that turn a group of individual musicians into a cohesive, harmonious ensemble.

Of course, none of this works without The Unspoken Language: Information and Communication. Think of the constant flow of information in an orchestra—the conductor's glance, the shared breath before a major chord, the subtle cues that keep hundreds of people perfectly in sync. In business, this is the nervous system—the clear reports, open channels, and honest conversations that ensure everyone knows the music, understands their part, and feels the rhythm of the organization.

Finally, there is Listening to the Playback: Monitoring. The best orchestras rehearse. They record themselves and listen back, not for praise, but for imperfections. They are constantly evaluating their own performance. Is a section dragging? Is the balance off? This is the act of monitoring. It's the relentless pursuit of perfection, the understanding that controls can weaken over time, and that continuous, critical listening is the only way to ensure the music never falters.

Ultimately, building a powerful internal control system isn't a bureaucratic chore. It's an act of profound creativity.

Recommend Internal Controls for Risk Management

Discuss the Committee of Sponsoring Organisations of the Treadway Commission (COSO) internal control and risk management framework

Imagine your organization isn't a building, but a ship setting sail on the vast, unpredictable ocean of commerce. Your mission is to reach profitable new lands, but the waters are teeming with risks—treacherous storms of market volatility, pirates of fraud, and the hidden reefs of regulatory trouble. How do you ensure your vessel not only survives but thrives? You need a master blueprint for building and sailing your ship. That blueprint is COSO.

The Wake of a Crisis: Why the Blueprint Was Drawn

Let's rewind to the 1980s. The business world was rocked by a series of spectacular shipwrecks—major companies capsizing due to financial fraud. The public, the investors, the crew—everyone was losing faith. They needed answers.

In response, five great maritime guilds of the modern age—think of them as the master shipwrights of accounting, finance, and auditing—banded together. The American Accounting Association (AAA), the AICPA, Financial Executives International (FEI), the Institute of Internal Auditors (IIA), and the Institute of Management Accountants (IMA) formed a special committee in 1985. Led by James C. Treadway, Jr., this "Treadway Commission" was tasked with a single, vital question: Why are these ships sinking, and how do we stop it?

Their findings gave birth to COSO's first great nautical chart in 1992: the Internal Control – Integrated Framework. This was the definitive guide to building a seaworthy vessel. Later, as the seas grew even more complex, COSO realized it wasn't enough to just have a strong ship; you needed a brilliant navigational strategy. So, they released the Enterprise Risk Management (ERM) Framework in 2004, a guide for charting the entire voyage. These frameworks became the gold standard, especially when laws like Sarbanes-Oxley (SOX) demanded that captains prove their ships were sound before sailing in public markets.

Blueprint #1: The Ship's Integrity (The Internal Control Framework)

This framework is about the ship itself—its design, its crew, and its onboard systems. It's built on five interconnected principles that ensure the vessel is strong enough for the journey.

The Crew's Code (Control Environment): This is the soul of the ship. It's the unwavering integrity of the captain and the officers, the "tone at the top." Does the crew believe in the mission? Is there a culture of discipline, ethics, and competence? If the captain is corrupt or the crew is mutinous, the strongest hull in the world won't matter. This is the foundation of trust upon which the entire voyage depends.

Charting the Waters (Risk Assessment): A good navigator never sails blind. This is the act of constantly scanning the horizon, studying the maps, and listening to the weather reports. Where are the storms brewing? What's the likelihood of encountering pirates? What hidden dangers lie beneath the waves? Before you can even plot a course, you must first understand the sea and all its perils.

Battening Down the Hatches (Control Activities): These are the specific actions the crew takes to handle the risks you've identified. It's assigning a lookout to the crow's nest, running lifeboat drills, and ensuring the cargo is securely tied down. It's the rule that two officers must hold keys to the ship's safe (segregation of duties). These are the practical, hands-on tasks that turn risk awareness into risk reduction.

The Flow of Information (Information and Communication): A silent ship is a doomed ship. The lookout's warning must reach the helm instantly. The captain's orders must be heard and understood by every sailor. The ship's log must be accurate for those back in port. This is the ship's nervous system, ensuring the right information gets to the right people, so they can make the right decisions at the right time.

The Constant Watch (Monitoring Activities): A ship requires constant upkeep. Is the hull still sound after that last storm? Are the sails beginning to fray? Is the crew still sharp, or are they growing complacent? This is the process of continuous evaluation—through regular inspections by the first mate (management) or a full review by seasoned experts (auditors)—to ensure all defenses are working as they should, day after day.

Blueprint #2: The Art of the Voyage (The ERM Framework)

If the first framework is about the ship, the ERM framework is about the journey. It integrates the reality of risk into the grand strategy of exploration and reward.

The Admiralty's Command (Governance and Culture): This sets the very purpose of the voyage. The board of directors and senior leadership define the mission and, crucially, how much risk the fleet is willing to endure to achieve it. This establishes the overarching risk culture for the entire enterprise.

Choosing a Destination (Strategy and Objective-Setting): You don't just sail; you sail somewhere. Here, you align your risk appetite with your strategic goals. You choose a destination (your objectives) knowing full well the potential dangers of the route. You wouldn't chart a course through hurricane season to deliver a small cargo of ice; the risk wouldn't justify the reward.

Navigating the Sea (Performance): This is the active part of the journey. You identify the specific icebergs and rogue waves that threaten your chosen course. You prioritize them and decide how to respond: Do you steer around the risk (avoid), plow through it prepared for damage (accept), reinforce the hull (reduce), or sail in a convoy (share)?

Learning from the Voyage (Review and Revision): No plan survives contact with the open ocean. This is the practice of looking back at the journey so far. Did you navigate that storm effectively? Was your map accurate? You constantly review your performance and revise your ERM approach, making your crew wiser and your ship better prepared for what lies ahead.

The Captain's Log (Information, Communication, and Reporting): This is about telling the story of your voyage. You report on the risks you faced, the culture of your crew, and your performance to the ship's owners (stakeholders) and the port authorities (regulators). This transparent communication builds trust and justifies future expeditions.

The Rewards of a Well-Sailed Ship

Adopting the COSO way isn't about getting bogged down in rules. It's about liberation. It's the freedom that comes from confidence.

A COSO-guided organization doesn't just avoid sinking; it sails with purpose. It navigates with greater efficiency, wasting less fuel and time. It builds a legendary reputation that attracts the best talent and the most loyal partners. It gives leadership the clear-eyed confidence to steer toward ambitious horizons, knowing their vessel is sound, their crew is ready, and their course is true.

In the end, COSO isn't just a framework; it's the collected wisdom of the world's best captains, distilled into a blueprint for greatness. It transforms your organization from a boat tossed about by circumstance into a master of the seas, capable of navigating any challenge and seizing every opportunity.

Assess control weakness, assess compliance failures, and recommend internal controls for risk management

The Art of Seeing Around Corners

Every organization, at its heart, is on a voyage. It's a ship sailing toward a destination, carrying precious cargo—its people, its reputation, and its future. But the sea is unpredictable. Storms of change gather on the horizon, hidden reefs of regulation lie just beneath the surface, and pirates of cybercrime are always watching for a vulnerable vessel. Thriving on this voyage isn't about avoiding the sea; it's about building a ship that can weather any storm. It's about learning to see around corners.

Finding the Cracks in the Hull: Where Weakness Hides

The strength of your ship is only as good as its weakest point. These weaknesses, or "control weaknesses," are the subtle cracks in the hull that can become catastrophic failures in a storm.

One of the most dangerous cracks is when one person holds too many keys. Imagine the ship's navigator also being the engine mechanic and the cook. If they make a mistake plotting the course, there's no one to notice because they're too busy in the galley. This is more than just a single point of failure; it's an invitation for disaster, born not always from malice, but from the simple, human reality of being overwhelmed and unwatched.

Another phantom menace is the "way we've always done it." When procedures live only in the minds of a few veterans and not in a clear, shared ship's log, chaos is the default. New crew members are left to guess, leading to inconsistent work and baffling mistakes. Trying to solve a problem becomes an archeological dig through memory and hearsay. This isn't a system; it's a collection of habits, and habits break easily under pressure.

We also see ships with brilliant, state-of-the-art equipment but a crew that has never been trained to use it. An employee who doesn't understand the 'why' behind a safety protocol is likely to see it as a bureaucratic hurdle, not a life-saving measure. Training isn't a box to be checked; it's the constant drilling that turns a group of individuals into a coordinated crew that can act instinctively when the alarms blare.

And then there's the ship itself. A vessel running on rusty, outdated technology is a sitting duck. An unpatched firewall is like a locked screen door—it looks like security, but it won't stop someone determined to get in. In a world where digital pirates are more sophisticated than ever, technological neglect isn't just risky; it's a deliberate choice to sail into dangerous waters unprotected.

But the most corrosive weakness starts in the captain's cabin. If leadership treats the rules of the sea as mere suggestions, that attitude will spread through the ship like a plague. A culture where shortcuts are celebrated and vigilance is mocked is a ship sailing toward an iceberg, with the band playing all the way.

Reading the Tides: Spotting Compliance Failures

Compliance is simply knowing the laws of the sea. These laws—from international regulations to the company's own internal code—are what separate a legitimate vessel from a rogue one. Ignoring them can get your ship seized.

Sometimes, a crew fails to comply because the star charts are old. Regulations are a living, breathing thing, constantly shifting. Sailing by last year's rules is like navigating by a constellation that no longer exists; you'll find yourself on the rocks, claiming you were following the map.

Worse yet is the captain who knowingly sails through protected waters to save fuel. This intentional disregard for the rules, this gamble that you won't get caught, is a poison to the organization's soul. The short-term win is an illusion, soon to be shattered by colossal fines and a reputation that sinks to the bottom.

Many ships have lookouts, but the captain never asks what they see. Without actively monitoring for compliance, violations become invisible. It's like having a speed limit with no radar. Rules without review are just decorations.

In our age, a ship's most valuable cargo is often its data. A data breach is the modern-day equivalent of being boarded by pirates who steal your manifests, your secrets, and your passengers' trust. The cost isn't just in regulatory fines; it's in the loss of faith from those you promised to protect.

Rigging the Ship for Success: Building a Culture of Control

So, how do we build a truly seaworthy vessel? We don't just patch the holes; we re-engineer the ship and retrain the crew.

First, give everyone a specific, vital role. The person who charts the course shouldn't be the one steering the ship. The one who stocks the provisions shouldn't be the only one who audits them. This separation of duties creates a natural system of checks and balances—a web of accountability where mistakes are caught early and collaboration is essential.

Next, write it down. Create a living, breathing ship's log—a single source of truth for every policy and procedure. Make it clear, make it accessible, and make it the standard by which all work is measured. This logbook doesn't stifle creativity; it provides the stable deck from which to innovate safely.

Turn training into a ritual. Conduct drills. Simulate storms. Make understanding the 'why' behind the rules as important as knowing the 'what'. An empowered, educated crew is your greatest asset. They are the human firewalls and the living alarm systems that technology can never replace.

Forge a stronger hull. Embrace technology as your armor. Keep your systems sharp, your defenses updated, and your data encrypted. Hire ethical hackers to probe your defenses, so you can find the cracks before the real pirates do.

Finally, it all comes back to the captain. Leadership must be the living embodiment of the ship's values. They must be on the deck, demonstrating vigilance, rewarding integrity, and fostering a culture where every single person feels responsible for the safety of the voyage.

The journey of risk management is a continuous loop of seeing, assessing, and strengthening. It's the art of building a resilient ship and fostering a brilliant crew, ready not just to survive the storm, but to harness its power and sail confidently toward the horizon.

Explanatory notes

This introduces the COSO framework as a comprehensive way of looking at internal controls in risk management. The objective is to get candidates to understand the key elements and know how to apply them in evaluating internal controls.

Beyond the Balance Sheet: The Secret to a Healthy Company

Every business owner, every leader, feels it. That low-grade hum of anxiety that comes with complexity. You build something you're proud of, a living, breathing organization with ambitions and a pulse. But with that life comes risk.

How do you protect it? How do you make sure it not only survives but thrives?

Forget dry acronyms and dense compliance manuals for a moment. Let's talk about organizational wellness. There's a philosophy for this, a way of seeing your company's inner workings, known in the business world as the COSO framework. But think of it less as a "framework" and more as the art and science of building a resilient, self-aware organization. It's the nervous system that connects your company's brain (its strategy) to its hands and feet (its daily operations).

It's not about creating a cage of rules. It's about cultivating the wisdom to navigate the unpredictable seas of commerce. It's about building an internal culture so robust that it can bend without breaking, adapt without panicking, and achieve its goals with integrity.

The Five Senses of a Healthy Organization

COSO is built on five interconnected ideas. They aren't checkboxes on a list; they are the vital signs of your company's health. To understand them is to understand the very character of your business.

1. The Heartbeat & Soul (Control Environment)

This is the character of your company. It's the "tone at the top," yes, but it's more than that—it's the culture you feel in the hallways, the unspoken understanding that integrity isn't just a poster on the wall. It's the leadership looking in the mirror and asking, "Who are we, and what do we stand for?" Is honesty a core value or just a talking point? Are people given responsibility and trusted to carry it out? This is your organization's moral compass. Without a strong, steady heartbeat of integrity, all other systems will eventually falter.

2. The Lookout in the Crow's Nest (Risk Assessment)

Every ship on the sea faces potential storms. A healthy organization doesn't pretend the sea is always calm; it posts a lookout. Risk assessment is the practice of scanning the horizon. What icebergs—economic shifts, new competitors, technological disruptions—are out there? And what about the creaks in your own hull—outdated processes, internal friction, or potential for human error? This isn't about fear; it's about awareness. It's the courage to look at your own vulnerabilities and the wisdom to map a course around the most dangerous threats, including the ever-present risk of fraud.

3. The Body's Reflexes and Muscle Memory (Control Activities)

These are the smart actions your organization takes without having to think about it. They are the reflexes and muscle memory that protect you. When you touch something hot, you pull your hand back instantly. Likewise, a well-controlled company has built-in actions. It's the rule that the person who approves an expense can't be the same person who pays it out. It's the automatic process of reconciling the bank account every month. It's locking the warehouse at night. These aren't burdensome procedures; they are the intelligent, ingrained habits that prevent stumbles, spills, and catastrophic falls.

4. The Nervous System (Information & Communication)

A body cannot function without a nervous system. Nerves carry signals from the farthest reaches of the body to the brain, and the brain's commands back out. This is the role of information and communication. Quality information is the lifeblood of awareness. It ensures that the brain (leadership) knows when a toe gets stubbed (a frontline problem). Communication is the network of nerves itself. Does information flow freely? Can an employee with a serious concern raise a flag without fear? When this system is healthy, everyone understands their role in the body, and the organization can react with speed and grace. When it's blocked, it's like a pinched nerve—painful and dysfunctional.

5. The Regular Health Check-Up (Monitoring Activities)

A healthy person pays attention to their body. They notice when they feel off. They go for regular check-ups. Monitoring is your company's commitment to self-reflection. Some of it is ongoing, like a manager reviewing their team's performance reports—a daily check of your vitals. Other check-ups are more formal, like an internal audit—the annual physical with a specialist. The goal isn't to find fault; it's to find opportunities for improvement. Monitoring asks, "Are we as healthy as we think we are? And if not, what's our prescription for getting better?" It ensures the organization's controls don't become obsolete, keeping it fit for the future.

Becoming the Organizational Doctor

When you use this lens to look at a company, you're not just an auditor; you're a diagnostician.

Start by checking the pulse (Control Environment). Does the leadership embody integrity? Then, scan the horizon (Risk Assessment). Does the company truly understand the dangers it faces? Test the reflexes (Control Activities). Are the safeguards real and are they working? Map the nervous system (Information & Communication). Is information flowing or getting trapped? Finally, schedule the follow-up (Monitoring). Is the organization learning and adapting?

By seeing your organization as a living entity, the COSO framework transforms from a rigid structure into a dynamic guide for nurturing corporate health. It's the path to building a company that isn't just profitable, but is also resilient, aware, and built to last.

Discuss Various Issues Relating to Internal Audit in Organizations

In the beating heart of any thriving organization, there's a quiet, steady pulse of integrity and insight. This is the world of internal audit, a function often misunderstood as a rigid group of box-tickers, but in reality, a team of strategic partners, storytellers, and organizational health coaches. They are the navigators who help a company not only play by the rules but also play its best game. Let's pull back the curtain on this vital function and see it for what it truly is: a dynamic force for improvement and a guardian of value.

The Many Faces of the Corporate Guardian

Internal audit is not a one-size-fits-all uniform; it's more like a closet full of specialized gear, each designed for a different terrain.

The Rulebook Guardian: A Compliance Audit

Think of the compliance auditor as the expedition's navigator, poring over maps of laws, regulations, and company policies. Their mission is to keep the ship off the rocks of legal trouble and out of the storms of reputational damage. Are we protecting customer data according to privacy laws like GDPR? Is our factory meeting environmental standards? Are we following the very code of conduct we wrote for ourselves? By meticulously checking these guideposts, they prevent costly fines and, more importantly, preserve the trust that is the currency of modern business.

The Corporate Detective: A Fraud Investigation

When something smells fishy—a strange blip in the financials, a tip from a concerned employee—the fraud investigators are called in. This isn't a routine check-up; it's a high-stakes detective story. Armed with forensic skills and a healthy dose of skepticism, they follow the money, interview witnesses, and sift through mountains of data to uncover the truth. Their goal isn't just to find the culprit and recover what was lost, but to understand how it happened and help the organization build stronger locks to prevent it from happening again. It's a delicate dance of discretion, precision, and the relentless pursuit of integrity.

The Value Hunter: A Value for Money (VFM) Audit

While others focus on doing things right, the VFM auditor asks a more profound question: Are we doing the right things? This isn't about being cheap; it's about being smart. They are the efficiency coaches, asking if every dollar, every hour of effort, is creating the most possible value. Is that multi-million dollar marketing campaign actually bringing in customers, or is it just a feel-good expense? Is our supply chain a sleek, efficient engine or a clunky, resource-guzzling machine? In the public sector, this means ensuring tax dollars are creating real community benefits. In the private sector, it's about maximizing the bang for every buck, pushing the organization to be leaner, more effective, and more successful.

The Big Picture Artist: A Management Audit

Zooming out from individual transactions, the management auditor looks at the entire masterpiece. They assess the very systems and strategies management uses to steer the ship. Is the leadership's vision clear? Is the crew rowing in sync? They might look at the HR department's ability to attract and retain top talent or evaluate the strategic planning process of a key division. They delve into culture, communication, and leadership effectiveness, seeking to strengthen the organizational scaffolding so that everyone can build towards a common goal. They ensure the company isn't just running, but running in the right direction.

The Auditor's Journey: A Process of Discovery

An audit isn't a random spot-check; it's a carefully planned expedition into the organization's landscape, following a map designed to lead to meaningful discoveries.

The Expedition Plan

The journey begins with a grand strategy session. Guided by an independent audit committee—think of them as the expedition's board of patrons—the auditors create an annual plan. This isn't a rigid itinerary but a dynamic map that marks the areas of highest risk and greatest opportunity. Once a specific audit is commissioned, a detailed program is drawn up, outlining the quest's objectives, the tools needed, and the timeline. Then, the fieldwork begins—the heart of the adventure, where auditors gather clues through interviews, observations, and deep dives into data, documenting their journey every step of the way.

Reading the Weather: Assessing Audit Risk

Before setting out, every good explorer assesses the risks. Auditors do the same, breaking down "audit risk"—the danger of getting it wrong—into three key elements:

Inherent Risk (The Terrain): This is the natural risk of the landscape itself. Cash, for example, is inherently more susceptible to disappearing than a factory building. Some industries, like fast-moving tech, are just naturally more treacherous and unpredictable.

Control Risk (The Gear): This is the risk that your equipment will fail. An organization's internal controls are its safety gear. If the controls are weak (like a frayed rope), the risk of a fall (a material error) is high. Strong controls mean the gear is reliable.

Detection Risk (The Explorer's Skill): This is the risk that the auditor, the explorer, will simply miss something important. This is the one risk the auditor can manage directly. If the terrain is treacherous and the gear is shoddy, the explorer must be incredibly careful and thorough, leaving no stone unturned to reduce the risk of missing a critical clue.

Connecting the Dots: The Art of Analytical Review

Great auditors are also great storytellers who can see a narrative in a sea of numbers. This is the magic of analytical review. It's about looking for patterns and asking "why?" Why did sales spike in the third quarter while production costs stayed flat? Why is one department's travel budget double that of a similar one? By comparing data against history, industry trends, and common sense, auditors can spot anomalies that point to hidden risks or opportunities. It's like a doctor reviewing a patient's vitals—one number might not mean much, but the trend line can tell a life-saving story.

The Anatomy of an Effective Audit Team

An audit function that truly adds value is built on a foundation of unshakeable principles.

The Spine of Independence, The Brains of the Operation, and the Fuel in the Tank

The non-negotiable bedrock of internal audit is independence. This is its spine. The team must report to the highest level of governance, the audit committee, ensuring they can speak truth to power without fear of reprisal from the management they are auditing. Just as crucial is the staffing—the brain and muscle. A modern audit team is a diverse crew of data scientists, IT wizards, operational experts, and financial gurus who bring a rich tapestry of skills to the table. Finally, even the best team is useless without adequate resourcing—the fuel in the tank. A proper budget for training, technology, and talent ensures the audit function can fulfill its crucial mandate, providing an incredible return on investment through reduced risk and enhanced performance.

The Final Chapter: The Audit Report

The culmination of the entire journey is the audit report. This document is not a verdict; it's a conversation starter, a roadmap for a better future.

From Findings to a Better Future

A great report tells a clear, compelling story. It begins with an Executive Summary—the movie trailer that grabs a busy executive's attention. The core of the report details the Findings, but it doesn't just state facts; it explains the impact. It answers the crucial "so what?" question, framing each weakness in terms of the risk it poses to the organization's goals.

For every finding, the report offers practical, actionable Recommendations—the proposed next chapter in the organization's story. But the story isn't a monologue. The most critical section is the Management Response and Action Plan. This is where management joins the conversation, agreeing to the findings and committing to a plan, with deadlines and responsible owners, to write a better future. This dialogue transforms the report from a critique into a collaborative blueprint for improvement, ensuring the journey of the audit leads to a stronger, more resilient organization.

Explanatory notes

In the vast, unpredictable ocean of modern commerce, every organization is a ship on a voyage. The mission is clear—to reach the shores of strategic success. But the seas are treacherous, filled with the sudden squalls of market volatility, the lurking pirates of cyber threats, and the shifting reefs of regulation. How does a captain—or a board of directors—navigate these dangers with confidence? They rely on their ship's surveyor: the internal audit function.

This isn't about having a critic on board, someone who just points out rust and fraying ropes. This is about having a master navigator and structural engineer rolled into one. The internal auditor is the one who goes below deck, tapping the hull to check its integrity, testing the rigging, and tasting the water in the casks. They provide the essential assurance that the vessel isn't just afloat, but truly seaworthy, ready to weather the coming storm and seize the opportunities that lie beyond the horizon. For any leader, especially those pursuing qualifications like CGMA, seeing internal audit through this lens changes everything.

The Surveyor's Allegiance: The Soul of the Audit

At the very heart of this role is a simple, non-negotiable principle: the surveyor works for the ship's captain (the board), not the crew. Imagine a surveyor who answers to the ship's cook. If the cook has been secretly selling rations, would the surveyor report the dwindling food supplies? Of course not. Independence is the surveyor's compass; it must always point true north, free from the magnetic interference of internal politics or operational pressures. This allows them to deliver unvarnished truth, based on hard evidence. Without this unwavering objectivity, their charts are worthless, and the captain is sailing blind.

The Surveyor's Toolkit: Competence and Resources

An independent spirit is vital, but it's useless without the right tools and expertise. You wouldn't ask a 17th-century mapmaker to navigate a modern supertanker. Today's surveyor needs more than a spyglass and a hunch. They need the digital equivalent of sonar and satellite imaging—advanced data analytics, deep knowledge of IT systems, and a sharp understanding of complex financial instruments. An under-equipped or undertrained audit team is like a lone surveyor sent to inspect an aircraft carrier with nothing but a flashlight. They might find a few scuff marks on the deck, but they will miss the hairline fracture in the engine block.

Charting the Entire Ship: The Importance of Scope

A surveyor who only inspects the sails and ignores the rudder is gambling with the entire voyage. Likewise, an internal audit that focuses solely on financial controls leaves the organization dangerously exposed. The modern ship faces threats from every direction. The surveyor's scope must be all-encompassing, from the strategic risk of a competitor launching a faster ship, to the operational risk of a weary crew making mistakes, to the emerging risk of a rogue AI trying to seize the helm. A narrow audit creates blind spots, and in a storm, a single blind spot can be the difference between reaching port and sinking without a trace.

The Navigator's Report: The Art of Communication

What good is discovering a critical vulnerability if the warning is delivered in cryptic code? The surveyor's findings must be translated into a clear, actionable chart for the captain and crew. A report that is too dense, too late, or too timid is just noise. The best auditors are storytellers; they don't just list problems, they paint a vivid picture: "This leak in the port bow will slow us by two knots, and if we hit heavy seas, it could flood the cargo hold. Here are three ways to patch it before we reach the cape." This is communication that inspires action and builds resilience.

A Trusted Voice, Not a Scolding Finger: The Human Connection

Ultimately, the surveyor and the crew are on the same ship, facing the same sea. A surveyor who barks orders and fosters an atmosphere of fear will find that the crew starts hiding problems. But one who builds relationships based on trust and a shared mission becomes an invaluable partner. When the crew trusts the surveyor, they will proactively point out the strange noise in the engine room or the unsettling sway in the mainmast. This collaborative spirit, where management sees audit as a resource for a safer, faster journey, is the wind in the sails of effective risk management.

These vital elements are not separate pillars; they are intertwined ropes in a single, strong cable. A surveyor with faulty tools (competence) will produce an incomplete map (scope). An unreadable map (communication) is useless, even if the information is correct. And if no one trusts the surveyor (relationships), the map will be ignored. If their loyalty is compromised (independence), the entire system collapses.

By seeing the internal audit not as a procedural necessity but as the ship's trusted surveyor, an organization can transform its relationship with risk. It stops simply hoping for safe passage and starts actively plotting a course to thrive, with the confidence that their vessel is sound, their charts are true, and they are ready for whatever the horizon holds.

Area D: Cyber Risk

Analyse Cyber Threats

Your Business Isn't Just a Business. It's a Living, Breathing Digital World

In this age of clicks and code, we've all become architects. We don't build with brick and mortar, but with data and networks. Your enterprise, whether it's a tiny startup or a global giant, is a bustling digital metropolis. Your data is the gold in the treasury, your operations are the busy market streets, and your reputation is the flag that flies from the highest tower.

But this city has no walls. It's built on the open plains of the internet, and threats are no longer a distant concern for the tech team in the basement—they are at the gates. Understanding the nature of these threats isn't just about protecting computers; it's about protecting the very soul of your creation.

The Unseen Tremors and the Aftershocks

A cyber risk is the ghost in the machine. It's the unsettling feeling that the digital ground beneath your feet is unstable. It's the potential for a sudden, violent earthquake to shake your city to its foundations, caused by anything from a misplaced key to a full-scale invasion.

The landscape of this threat is a shapeshifter. The monsters of yesterday are today's forgotten legends, replaced by new, more cunning beasts that learn from our defenses.

This isn't a static war; it's a relentless, dynamic dance with an invisible partner who is always trying to lead.

When the quake hits, the damage isn't just about cracked pavement or a toppled statue. It's about the city going dark. It's the moment the bridges collapse, the supply lines are cut, and the marketplace falls silent. The financial cost is a gaping wound—the price of rebuilding, the tributes paid to attackers, the lawsuits from citizens whose homes were lost. But the deeper wound is the loss of faith. When the people believe their city is no longer safe, they leave. That loss of trust is a poison in the well, contaminating your legacy long after the rubble has been cleared.

The Rogues' Gallery: A Field Guide to Digital Invaders

The threats to your digital world are varied and imaginative, each with its own signature style of chaos. Knowing your enemy is the first step to fortifying your defenses.

Sabotage from the Shadows (Malware)

Think of malware not as software, but as a hostile lifeform seeking to infect your city.

Viruses: Digital graffiti artists who tag your most important blueprints, corrupting them until they're useless.

Worms: Self-replicating phantoms that don't need an invitation. They find a crack in the aqueduct system and multiply until they've clogged every pipe, bringing the entire city's water supply (your network) to a standstill.

Ransomware: A dragon that swoops in, locks your entire food supply in an impenetrable vault, and leaves a note demanding tribute for its return. Your city starves until you pay.

Spyware: An invisible eavesdropper hiding in the council chambers, listening to every secret, recording every private conversation, and reporting it all back to your enemies.

Exploiting the Architecture (Application Attacks)

Sometimes, the danger isn't an invader, but a flaw in your city's own design.

SQL Injection: This is like a stranger walking up to your city's archive keeper and whispering a command in a forgotten language that compels the keeper to hand over the most secret scrolls.

Cross-Site Scripting (XSS): Imagine an attacker carving a mesmerizing, hypnotic symbol onto the wall of the public square. Anyone who looks at it falls into a trance and willingly hands over the keys to their home.

Broken Authentication: This is the simplest and most human flaw of all. It's the guard who fell asleep and left the side gate swinging open in the wind.

The Faces Behind the Mask (Hackers)

Who are these invaders? Their motives are as diverse as their methods.

The Cyber-Syndicate: Organized criminals driven by one thing: profit. They are the mob bosses of the digital age, stealing gold, running extortion rackets, and trading secrets on a hidden black market.

The Crown's Spies: Agents of a rival nation-state. Their mission isn't wealth, but power. They conduct espionage, steal industrial secrets, and map out your city's defenses for a future, larger attack.

The Hacktivists: Revolutionaries with a cause. They aren't trying to steal your gold; they're trying to make a statement. They hijack your town crier, hang protest banners from your towers, or clog the city gates to disrupt your way of life.

The Traitor Within: The most heartbreaking threat. A disgruntled citizen, a careless official, or a former guardsman with a grudge. They don't need to breach the walls; they were given the keys.

When the Foundations Crack: The Real Cost of an Open Gate

A vulnerability is a crack in your city wall, a poorly drawn map, a secret tunnel you never knew existed. The crack itself is harmless. The danger is what might crawl through it. When it's exploited, the consequences ripple through every part of your world.

The Great Stillness (Downtime): The markets fall silent. The factories stop churning. The ships are frozen in the harbor. Every moment of this stillness is a moment of lost commerce, lost progress, and growing desperation. It's the sound of your city dying.

A Tarnished Flag (Reputational Loss): Trust is the currency of any great city. Once news spreads that your walls are weak and your treasury has been plundered, that trust evaporates. Allied cities will reconsider their treaties. Traveling merchants will reroute their caravans. Your city's name becomes a synonym for weakness.

The Exodus (Customer Flight): The citizens whose homes were ransacked and whose security was violated will not stay. They will pack their belongings and journey to the neighboring city—the one known for its strong walls and vigilant guards. This exodus bleeds your city of its lifeblood, leaving it a ghost of its former self.

The Reckoning (Legal and Industry Consequences): The attack may be over, but the judgment is just beginning.

Tributes and Fines: The great councils of nations (like the GDPR) will demand heavy tribute for your failure to protect your citizens.

The People's Court: Your own citizens will rise up in class-action lawsuits, demanding restitution for the harm you allowed to befall them.

Excommunication: Powerful guilds (like PCI DSS for finance or HIPAA for health) may cast you out, forbidding others from trading with you and leaving your city isolated and impoverished.

Ultimately, protecting your digital enterprise is an act of civic duty. It requires looking beyond code and servers and seeing the living, breathing world you've built. It demands vigilance, foresight, and the understanding that you are not just a manager or an employee; you are the guardian of a city, and its future rests in your hands.

Explanatory notes

The Ghost in the Machine

Every business, from the corner coffee shop to the global conglomerate, has a shadow. It's an unseen partner that watches every transaction, reads every email, and tests every lock. This shadow is the ever-present risk of a cyber threat, and ignoring it is like pretending the reflection in the mirror isn't real. It's not a matter of if the shadow will strike, but how you'll stand up when it does.

The Cracks in Our Digital Castle

Our organizations are not sterile fortresses of code and servers; they are living, breathing ecosystems. And like any living thing, they have vulnerabilities.

The most profound weakness isn't in a line of code; it's in the human heart. We are the soul of our companies, but we are also the most susceptible. Think of Sarah in accounting, who gets an email that looks exactly like one from her boss, asking for an urgent transfer. Her desire to be helpful becomes the key that unlocks the vault. We call it "social engineering," but it's as old as time: a con artist's whisper. We are wired to trust, and that trust is the primary target. Every employee without training is a potential unlocked door. Every lost laptop or disgruntled team member is a ghost story waiting to be told.

Then there's the digital skeleton of our operations—the technology itself. Imagine running your business in a building with crumbling foundations and windows that don't quite shut. That's what using outdated software is like. Hackers aren't always geniuses breaking new ground; often, they're simply burglars walking through a door someone forgot to patch months ago. The complexity of our modern world—cloud servers, personal phones, a dozen apps for everything—creates a maze of potential entry points, a thousand tiny cracks in the armor.

Beyond people and machines are our habits, our muscle memory as an organization. What happens when the alarm bells finally ring? Do we have a fire drill, or do we descend into chaos? An missing incident response plan is the difference between a controlled fire and a city-leveling inferno. Backing up data isn't just a chore; it's the blueprint for rebuilding your world after it turns to ash.

And what about our neighborhood? We don't exist in a vacuum. Our suppliers, partners, and vendors are all connected to us. Their security is our security. A breach in a trusted partner's system can become a secret tunnel leading straight into your own throne room.

A Rogues' Gallery of Digital Threats

The dangers that lurk in the digital ether are as varied as the villains in a comic book, each with their own twisted motive.

There's the digital mugger: ransomware. This brute force attacker doesn't sneak; it kicks down the door, locks up your most precious possessions—your data—and leaves a ransom note on the screen. It preys on your desperation.

Meet the master of disguise: phishing. This threat is a wolf in sheep's clothing. It arrives as a trusted email, a helpful text message, or a friendly phone call, manipulating you into handing over the keys to your kingdom.

Then there's the overwhelming mob: the Denial of Service (DoS) attack. It's not about stealing anything. It's about creating chaos, flooding your front door with so much traffic that legitimate customers and employees can't get in. It's the digital equivalent of a permanent protest blocking your business.

The most fearsome may be the silent ghost: the Advanced Persistent Threat (APT). This is no smash-and-grab. This is a spy who slips in undetected and lives within your walls for months, or even years, quietly mapping your network, learning your secrets, and siphoning off your most valuable intellectual property.

And we can't forget the betrayer from within. Whether driven by greed, revenge, or simple carelessness, the insider threat is uniquely painful because it comes from a place of trust.

These attacks are launched by a diverse cast of characters. Cybercriminals are the mercenaries, driven by profit. Nation-states are the spymasters, playing a global game of espionage and power. Hacktivists are the zealots, using digital disruption to broadcast their ideology. In every case, you are the target.

The Aftermath: More Than Just Lost Data

A successful cyberattack is a corporate earthquake. The initial shock is just the beginning; the aftershocks can ripple for years.

First comes the financial hemorrhage. There's the potential ransom, the staggering cost of rebuilding systems, the eye-watering regulatory fines, and the legal battles. But it's also the deafening silence of lost business as your operations grind to a halt.

Then comes the shattered reputation. Trust is a fragile crystal, built over years and shattered in an instant. A public breach tells your customers that you couldn't protect them. That stain is hard to wash out. It poisons relationships with partners, spooks investors, and gives your competitors the ultimate talking point.

Finally, there's the theft of your company's soul: its intellectual property. For a company built on a brilliant idea, a secret formula, or a groundbreaking design, losing that isn't just a setback; it's the end of the story.

In this digital age, cybersecurity is not an IT issue; it's a leadership issue. It's about cultivating a culture of vigilance, where every person understands their role as a guardian. It's not about building a perfect, impenetrable fortress. It's about being resilient, adaptable, and ready, so that when the shadow moves, you're prepared to step into the light.

Review Cyber Security Processes

Beyond the Buzzwords: The Soul of Digital Trust

In our hyper-connected world, we toss around terms like "cybersecurity" as if they were simple items on a checklist. But behind the jargon lies something deeply human: trust. Cybersecurity isn't just about protecting data; it's about upholding the promises we make to our customers, our partners, and ourselves. This trust is built on three foundational pillars—the very soul of a secure digital presence.

1. The Promise of Secrecy (Confidentiality)
Think of this as the sanctity of a whispered secret. It's the assurance that private conversations stay private and sensitive blueprints remain unseen by rival architects. Confidentiality is our digital vow to protect our company's crown jewels—be it a customer's personal story, a secret recipe, or next quarter's financial strategy. When this promise is broken, it's more than a data leak; it's a betrayal that can shatter reputations and crumble the bedrock of a business.

2. The Promise of Truth (Integrity)
This is the guarantee that the map we're reading is accurate. Integrity ensures that the data we rely on to make critical decisions hasn't been subtly warped or maliciously altered. Imagine a world where numbers lie—where a financial report is invisibly doctored, or an engineering schematic is corrupted just enough to cause catastrophic failure. A loss of integrity creates a funhouse mirror effect, where we can no longer trust what we see. It's the difference between a solid foundation and digital quicksand.

3. The Promise of Access (Availability)
This promise is simple: the lights will be on when you need them. Availability means that when an authorized user needs to access a tool or a piece of information, it's there for them, ready and waiting. When availability fails, the digital doors are slammed shut. Your e-commerce site goes dark on Black Friday, your production line halts because the system is down, or your team is paralyzed, unable to access the data they need to do their jobs. It's the digital equivalent of a "Closed" sign hanging on the door of a 24/7 business.

Building the Digital Fortress: A Strategy of Defense

To keep these promises, we can't just hope for the best. We must build a defense. Think of your organization not as an office building, but as a living, breathing digital fortress. A modern fortress isn't just about high walls; it has a multi-layered defense system designed to protect, detect, and respond.

Layer 1: The Fortress Walls (Protection)

This is your proactive defense—building your walls high and your gates strong before the battle begins.

Firewalls are your vigilant gatekeepers, inspecting everyone and everything that tries to enter or leave your network, turning away known troublemakers.

Encryption is a form of digital alchemy. It transforms your most precious data into an unreadable secret language, making it worthless to any thief who manages to snatch it without the magic key.

Access Controls, like multi-factor authentication (MFA), are the secret handshakes and retinal scans of the digital world, ensuring that only the right people get through the right doors.

Security Training is about turning every employee into a watchful guard. You can have the strongest gates in the world, but they're useless if someone inside is tricked into handing over the keys. This transforms your weakest link into your first line of defense.

Layer 2: The Watchful Sentinels (Detection)

Even the strongest walls can be scaled. That's why you need sentinels—systems that are constantly scanning the horizon for signs of trouble.

Intrusion Detection Systems (IDS) are your digital tripwires and silent alarms, alerting you the moment an intruder steps where they shouldn't.

A Security Information and Event Management (SIEM) system is your central watchtower. It doesn't just watch one gate; it has eyes and ears everywhere. It listens to the whispers from servers, the footsteps across the network, and the logs from every application. By weaving these disparate threads together, it can spot the subtle, coordinated patterns of a sophisticated attack that would otherwise go unnoticed. It's what separates the rustle of leaves from the footsteps of an intruder.

Layer 3: The Elite Response Team (Response)

When the alarm finally blares, chaos is the enemy. A swift, coordinated response is everything.

Your Incident Response Plan (IRP) is the battle plan you practice in peacetime. It replaces panic with purpose, outlining every step from sounding the alarm to containing the threat and recovering.

Disaster Recovery (DR) and Business Continuity (BC) plans are your strategies for surviving the siege. They ensure that even if one part of your fortress is burning, the mission-critical functions of your kingdom can carry on. This is how you keep the lights on for your customers, even in the darkest hours.

Forensic Analysis is about playing detective after the fight. By piecing together what happened, you not only bring the culprits to light but also learn how to reinforce your defenses so the same attack can never succeed again.

The Power of the Command Center: Centralizing Your Defenses

A scattered defense is a weak defense. An army with a hundred different commanders giving conflicting orders is doomed to fail. To be truly effective, a fortress needs a central command center.

Centralized Management: The Conductor's Baton

Imagine an orchestra where every musician plays from a different sheet of music at their own tempo. The result is noise. Centralized management is the conductor who ensures everyone plays the same symphony in perfect harmony. From a single console, a unified team can:

Enforce one security policy across the entire organization, eliminating weak spots and inconsistencies.

Deploy patches and updates to every single device simultaneously, closing vulnerabilities before they can be exploited.

Manage every user's identity and access from one place, ensuring that when someone leaves the organization, all their keys are immediately and completely revoked.

This isn't just about efficiency; it's about creating a single, coherent, and powerful defensive posture.

Centralized Monitoring: The View from the Watchtower

This is the power of bringing all your intelligence into one place. Your Security Operations Center (SOC) is the team in the command center, looking at the holistic view provided by your SIEM. They aren't just watching one wall; they are watching the entire kingdom.

By integrating data from every corner of your digital fortress with threat intelligence from the outside world, this team gains something akin to foresight. They can spot a known enemy's banner on the horizon long before they reach the gates. This ability to see the whole picture transforms security from a reactive scramble into a proactive, intelligence-driven operation, drastically cutting down the time it takes to spot and neutralize a threat.

Ultimately, mastering cybersecurity is about more than just technology. It's about building a culture of vigilance and resilience. For leaders and financial stewards, it's about understanding that a strong defense is no longer a cost center—it is the essential foundation that enables innovation, protects value, and preserves the sacred trust upon which your entire enterprise is built.

Explanatory notes

The Soul of Your Digital Kingdom: A New Vision for Cybersecurity

Forget about frameworks and firewalls for a moment. Think of your organization as a living, breathing kingdom. It has a culture, treasures to protect, citizens to serve, and a reputation to uphold in the wider world. In this digital age, your cybersecurity strategy isn't just an IT checklist; it is the grand strategy for the defense and prosperity of your realm.

The King's Decree: What We Swear to Protect

Before you can build your walls or train your soldiers, the crown must declare what truly matters. These aren't just goals; they are the sacred vows that give your kingdom purpose.

Protecting the Crown Jewels: Every kingdom has its treasure. Is it the secret recipe for a legendary product (your intellectual property)? Is it the trust and personal stories of your populace (customer data)? Is it the gold in the royal treasury (your financial systems)? Your first and most solemn vow is to identify these priceless assets and guard them above all else. They are the reason your kingdom exists.

Keeping the Heart of the City Beating: An attack isn't just about theft; it's about paralysis. A dragon might not steal your gold, but its fire can burn the fields and stop the harvest. Your objective must be resilience—the ability to keep the markets open, the water flowing, and the citizens working, even while under siege. It's about having a plan to rebuild the wall even as the arrows fly.

The Three Sacred Oaths of Security: At the core of your defense lies a trinity of principles, the vows every guard must take:

The Whisper's Pact (Confidentiality): Secrets entrusted to the crown must remain secret. Private conversations stay private. This is the promise that sensitive information is for your eyes only.

The Scribe's Oath (Integrity): The royal scrolls must speak the truth. Every ledger, map, and historical record must be pure and untampered with, ensuring the data that runs your kingdom is accurate and trustworthy.

The Open Gates (Availability): While we guard against our enemies, the gates must always open for our own citizens. Your people must be able to access the tools, information, and services they need, whenever they need them.

Honoring the Laws of the Land: Your kingdom does not exist in a vacuum. There are treaties, alliances, and ancient laws that govern the world (like GDPR, HIPAA, and others). To defy them is to invite war, crippling tariffs (fines), and exile from the global community. Compliance isn't a burden; it's diplomacy and survival.

A Culture of Vigilance: Every Citizen a Watchman: The strongest walls are useless if a spy is invited in through the front gate. Your people—from the high council to the newest apprentice—are your first and most vital line of defense. Your goal is to foster a culture where security is second nature. You must train every citizen to spot a disguised threat, to question a strange request, and to understand that they are the true guardians of the realm.

Charting New Worlds, Securely: A kingdom that only looks inward will eventually stagnate and fade. Growth, innovation, and exploration (digital transformation) are essential. The goal of security, then, is not to be the anchor holding the ship in port. It is to be the master navigator and shipwright, allowing your vessel to sail into new and exciting waters, confident that its hull is strong and its crew is ready for any storm.

The Kingdom's Arsenal: Your Tools of Defense

Once your vows are made clear, you must equip your kingdom. These are the controls you use to enforce your will and protect your people, blending powerful magic (technology) with the unshakeable wisdom of your court (policy).

The Royal Engineer's Toolkit (Technical Controls)

The Great Walls and Gatekeepers (Firewalls): These are your primary defense, inspecting all who seek to enter or leave your kingdom's network and denying entry to known enemies.

The Sentinels on the Watchtower (IDPS): These eagle-eyed scouts constantly monitor the landscape for suspicious movements. They don't just watch; they sound the alarm and can launch the first volley of arrows to stop an intruder in their tracks.

The Royal Scribe's Cipher (Encryption): A powerful spell that turns your most precious messages into an unreadable script. Even if a scroll is stolen, its contents are meaningless without the secret decoding key.

The King's Two Seals (MFA): To access the most sensitive chambers, a simple key (password) is not enough. One must also present the King's signet ring or a secret word—a second factor that proves you are who you claim to be.

The Master Masons and Patch-Work (VulnerabilityManagement): Your defenses must be maintained. These are the master builders who constantly inspect the walls for cracks and weaknesses, patching them before they can be exploited by a clever foe.

The Grand Strategy Map (SIEM): In the central war room, reports from every watchtower, patrol, and city guard are collected on a single map. This allows you to see the patterns in an enemy's movements and anticipate their grand strategy before they strike.

The Inner Moats and Wards (NetworkSegmentation): You don't build just one wall. You build walls within walls. By dividing your kingdom into isolated wards, you ensure that if one section is breached, the enemy cannot simply roam freely through the entire castle.

The Secret Vault and the Seed Bank (BackupandRecovery): Should the worst happen—a fire, a flood, a devastating attack—you have a secret, untouched vault where duplicates of your treasures and the seeds to regrow your harvest are stored. This is your guarantee that the kingdom can always be rebuilt.

The Wisdom of the Royal Court (Administrative Controls)

The Royal Decrees and Written Law (Policies): These are the clear, written rules of the land that every citizen and noble must follow—how to handle information, how to challenge a stranger, and what to do when the war horn sounds.

The War Horns and Battle Plans (IncidentResponsePlan): When an attack happens, chaos is the enemy. You must have a pre-rehearsed plan that dictates who does what, ensuring a swift, coordinated, and effective defense to minimize damage.

Vetting the Foreign Mercenaries (VendorRiskManagement): You often hire outsiders (third-party vendors) to aid your kingdom. You must carefully investigate their loyalties and their own defenses, for their weakness could become your downfall.

The System of Royal Keys (AccessControl): The stable hand does not need the key to the treasury. The principle is simple: grant each person only the keys they absolutely need to do their job, and no more. This is the law of least privilege.

By weaving these elements together—a noble purpose, powerful tools, and shared wisdom—you transform cybersecurity from a cold, technical discipline into the living, breathing heart of your kingdom's defense. You build a realm that is not only secure but resilient, prosperous, and ready for the future.

Discuss Cyber Security Tools and Techniques

The Digital Ghost Whisperers: A Guide to Forensic Analysis

Forget the yellow tape and chalk outlines. Today's most compelling crime scenes are invisible, woven into the ones and zeros of our digital lives. Forensic analysis is the art of listening to the ghosts in the machine. It's about coaxing secrets from silent hard drives and tracing whispers across networks to piece together a story someone tried to erase. This isn't just for nabbing hackers; it's about understanding how a system broke, what happened during a data breach, and ensuring it never happens again.

System Analysis: Reading a Computer's Diary

Every computer keeps a diary. It's a scattered, messy, and often cryptic journal of its life, and a system-level analyst is the one who knows how to read it. We're not just looking at files; we're examining the machine's soul.

We pour over operating system logs, which dutifully note every login, every program launched, every virtual door opened. On Windows, the Registry is a treasure trove—a sprawling database of settings that acts like the computer's memory, revealing what software once lived there, which USB drives paid a visit, and how the user customized their world. We dig through digital clutter like temporary files and browser caches, which often hold forgotten fragments of web pages, documents, and images. Even the Recycle Bin is a first stop, the place where secrets are often thrown but not forgotten. This is how we reconstruct a timeline, understanding not just what happened on a computer, but the rhythm and habits of the person who used it.

Storage Analysis: The Digital Archaeology Dig

This is where we put on our gloves and get our hands dirty. Storage analysis is a deep dive into the digital graveyard of hard drives, SSDs, and flash drives. Hitting "delete" doesn't destroy a file; it just removes the signpost pointing to it. The data itself often lies undisturbed, like a lost city buried under sand.

Using specialized tools, we create a perfect, bit-for-bit copy of a drive—a digital fossil record. Then, the real dig begins. We sift through unallocated space, the digital wilderness where old files once lived, searching for recoverable data. We even examine slack space, the tiny leftover bits of storage at the end of a file, which can contain ghosts of whatever data was there before. It's a painstaking process of unearthing digital remains, piecing together shattered documents and deleted photos to reveal evidence someone thought was gone forever.

Network Analysis: Following the Breadcrumbs Across the Web

If storage analysis is an archaeological dig, network analysis is like being an air traffic controller for the internet. We watch the incredible flow of data packets zipping across a network, looking for rogue flights and suspicious conversations.

We capture and analyze this traffic, decoding the conversations between computers. Each packet tells a story: where it came from, where it's going, and what it's carrying. By piecing them together, we can reconstruct file transfers, see what websites were visited, and identify strange connections to unknown servers. We're hunting for Indicators of Compromise (IOCs)—the tell-tale signatures of malware or the digital footprints of an attacker. This gives us the big picture, allowing us to map an intruder's journey through the network and see exactly what they came for.

The Digital Autopsy: Inside the Mind of Malware

Malware—viruses, ransomware, spyware—is like a digital parasite. Malware analysis is the autopsy we perform to understand how it lives, how it attacks, and how to kill it. By dissecting these malicious programs, we learn to build stronger defenses and anticipate the enemy's next move.

Reverse Engineering: Thinking Like the Enemy

At the heart of this dark science is reverse engineering. It's the process of taking a finished piece of malicious software and deconstructing it, piece by piece, to understand its sinister design without ever seeing the original blueprints (the source code).

Imagine being a bomb disposal expert, carefully taking apart a complex device to understand its trigger mechanism. Analysts work in secure, isolated "sandboxes" to let the malware run wild without harming anything, observing its every move. This highly specialized skill requires a deep understanding of how software and operating systems truly work. It's about learning to think like the malware's creator to uncover its secrets.

Decompilation & Disassembly: Translating the Malware's Language

To understand the malware's intent, we have to learn its language.

Decompilation is like using a universal translator. It takes the computer's native language—raw machine code—and attempts to translate it back into a higher-level programming language that's easier for a human to read. The translation isn't always perfect, but it provides a clear overview of the malware's logic and overall goal, revealing the "what" and "why" of the attack.

Disassembly is a much more literal translation. It converts the machine code into assembly language, the most basic, human-readable set of instructions for the computer's processor. It's like reading the malware's moment-to-moment thoughts. While far more complex, this granular view shows us exactly how the malware operates, step-by-step, giving us the precise knowledge needed to neutralize it.

The Ethical Hacker: Breaking In to Keep Others Out

How do you know if your fortress is secure? You hire a master locksmith to try and break in. That's penetration testing (or pen testing) in a nutshell. It's a simulated, authorized cyberattack designed to find and fix security holes before the real bad guys do.

Phase 1: Network Discovery (Casing the Joint)

The first step is reconnaissance. A pen tester meticulously maps the target's digital landscape, just like a burglar casing a mansion. They use sophisticated tools to scan for every active computer, open port, and running service. They're creating a detailed blueprint of the network, identifying every potential door and window. The more they know about the layout, the easier it will be to find a way in.

Phase 2: Vulnerability Probing (Rattling the Doorknobs)

With the map in hand, the pen tester starts looking for weaknesses. This is the vulnerability probing phase, where they gently rattle the digital doorknobs and check the window latches. They use automated scanners and manual techniques to find unpatched software, weak passwords, and common configuration mistakes. They're not breaking anything yet; they're just finding the cracks in the armor.

Phase 3: Exploiting Vulnerabilities (Picking the Lock)

This is where the fun begins. The pen tester now attempts to exploit the weaknesses they found. Their goal isn't to steal or damage anything, but to prove that the vulnerability is real. They might use a known exploit or craft a custom one to gain access, elevate their privileges, or show they can access sensitive data. It's the equivalent of picking the lock and leaving a polite note on the kitchen table that says, "You should probably fix this." This concrete proof is what organizations need to understand their risk and take action.

The Art of Digital Fortification: Building Secure Software

True security isn't a feature you add at the end; it's an philosophy woven into every stage of creation. Software security is about building applications that are inherently resilient, like constructing a castle with defense in mind from the very first blueprint. This is done in layers, creating a defense that's strong from its core to its highest tower.

Tier 1: Secure Coding (The DNA of the Code)

This is the bedrock. It's about teaching developers to write code that is naturally resistant to attack. This means obsessing over things like input validation (never trusting user data) and avoiding common pitfalls like buffer overflows. It's like ensuring the very bricks and mortar of your castle are forged with strength and integrity. This tier is all about building security into the software's DNA through training, code reviews, and smart practices.

Tier 2: SAST & DAST (The Automated Inspectors)

Once the code is written, it's time for inspection.

Static Application Security Testing (SAST) is the inspector who reads your blueprints. It analyzes the raw source code without running it, looking for known structural flaws and security vulnerabilities before the application is even built.

Dynamic Application Security Testing (DAST) is the inspector who stress-tests the finished building. It attacks the running application from the outside, just like a real hacker would, to find weaknesses that only appear when the system is live.

Tier 3: Penetration Testing & Vulnerability Management (The Professional Siege Team)

This is where you bring in the experts. Penetration testing provides a creative, human-driven attack to find the complex, logic-based flaws that automated tools miss. But security isn't a one-time test. Vulnerability management is the ongoing process of having a dedicated watchman who constantly patrols the castle walls, looking for new cracks, assessing their danger, and ensuring they are promptly repaired.

Tier 4: RASP (The Self-Defending Castle)

This is where the castle comes alive. Runtime Application Self-Protection (RASP) embeds security directly into the application, giving it a kind of immune system. RASP watches for attacks from the inside and can actively defend itself in real-time. If it detects a malicious attack, it can block it instantly, terminate the attacker's session, and send an alert. It's a castle that doesn't just have walls; it has walls that can fight back.

Tier 5: Threat Modeling & Security Architecture (The Master Architect)

This is the highest level of strategic defense. Before laying a single stone, the master architect performs threat modeling, considering every possible threat—from dragons to invading armies—and designing defenses accordingly. Security architecture is the master blueprint itself, integrating security into the very fabric of the system. It dictates where to build the moats, how high to raise the walls, and where to place the watchtowers. It's a holistic approach that ensures the castle isn't just secure, but was born to be secure from its very inception.

Explanatory notes

Think of your company not as a building, but as a living, breathing body. Its data is the lifeblood, coursing through digital veins, powering every decision, every transaction, every connection. In this new world, the threats we face aren't burglars or vandals; they are microscopic, invisible pathogens—digital viruses, parasites, and toxins that can bring the entire organism to a grinding halt. Managing cyber risk, then, isn't just an IT chore. It's a practice of corporate wellness, a discipline dedicated to keeping this digital body alive and thriving.

The Annual Check-Up: A Diagnosis of Your Digital Health

You wouldn't wait for a heart attack to see a doctor. So why wait for a catastrophic breach to understand your digital health? The first step is always diagnosis—a deep, honest look under the hood. This is more than just taking your temperature; it's a full workup.

Frameworks like the NIST Cybersecurity Framework or ISO 27001 act as our diagnostic charts. They force us to ask the fundamental questions a doctor would: Where are your vital organs—the servers holding your crown jewels, the systems that cannot fail? What are your pre-existing conditions—the outdated software, the unpatched vulnerabilities, the weak points in your anatomy? And what plagues are sweeping the globe that you might be susceptible to? This isn't a scare tactic; it's the essential act of knowing your body, its strengths, and its frailties.

Building a Digital Immune System: The Art of Staying Well

Once you understand your health, the focus shifts to preventing illness. This is about building a powerful, reflexive immune system, combining biological defenses with conscious, healthy choices.

First, you have the body's innate defenses—your technical controls. Your firewall is the skin, a semi-permeable barrier that keeps most pathogens out. Antivirus software acts as your white blood cells, hunting down and neutralizing invaders that manage to slip past. Think of encryption as a secret language spoken only by your own cells, making your data complete gibberish to any foreign body. And multi-factor authentication? That's like requiring a unique DNA signature to access a vital organ, making a stolen key (or password) useless on its own.

But a strong body isn't just about biology; it's about lifestyle. These are your policy and process controls. Clear security policies are the nutritional guidelines that tell everyone what's healthy to consume and what's poison. Employee training, especially on spotting phishing scams, is like teaching your body to recognize and reject junk food. An incident response plan is knowing the number for the ambulance before you have a stroke. And managing your vendors? That's ensuring the partners you connect with are washing their hands, so they don't pass their germs on to you.

Listening to Your Body: Detecting Sickness Early

Despite our best efforts, we all get sick. The key is to catch it early, to notice the subtle signs before a common cold becomes pneumonia. This is the art of detection.

A Security Information and Event Management (SIEM) system is your central nervous system. It receives billions of tiny signals—a nerve twitch here, a slight temperature spike there—from every corner of your digital body. Using powerful analytics and AI, it pieces together these seemingly random symptoms to spot a pattern, alerting you to the fever or the infection brewing deep within the network long before it becomes critical.

Vulnerability management is your routine screening. Regular scans are the blood tests that check for known markers of disease. But penetration testing goes a step further. It's the stress test on the treadmill, where ethical hackers, like specialized doctors, safely push your systems to their limits to see where the weaknesses lie. They find the hairline fracture before it shatters under pressure.

The Emergency Room & Rehabilitation: Responding to Trauma:

When the alarms blare and an attack is successful, you enter the emergency room. This is where a clear head and a well-rehearsed plan can mean the difference between a full recovery and a fatality.

Your incident response and recovery plan is the trauma team. It's a choreographed dance of specialists who know exactly what to do: stop the bleeding (contain the breach), perform surgery (eradicate the threat), and then conduct a post-mortem (forensic analysis) to understand what happened and prevent a relapse. The immediate goal is to stabilize the patient.

From there, you move to rehabilitation. Business Continuity and Disaster Recovery plans are the physical therapy that helps your organization learn to walk again, to regain strength, and to get back to full function after a devastating blow. And finally, cyber insurance is your health insurance. It won't stop the heart attack, but it provides the financial resources to pay for the expensive surgery, the long recovery, and the lost income, ensuring the trauma doesn't lead to bankruptcy.

The Path to Wellness: A Holistic Journey:

True cybersecurity isn't a single tool or a one-time fix. It's a holistic commitment to lifelong wellness. It's the seamless integration of a resilient immune system, a sensitive nervous system, healthy daily habits, and a world-class emergency response team.

This is a continuous journey, a cycle of diagnosis, prevention, detection, and response. It requires leadership from the very top—a board and C-suite who understand that in our modern world, digital health is business health. By embracing this mindset, we can build organizations that are not just defended, but are truly resilient, ready to face the complexities of the digital age with strength, awareness, and confidence.

Evaluate Cyber Risk Reporting

Crafting Your Cyber Story: Essential Chapters for a Compelling Risk Report

Forget the dry binders and the soul-crushing compliance checklists. A truly great cyber risk report isn't a document; it's a story. It's the living, breathing narrative of your organization's journey through the wild, unpredictable digital frontier. It's a story that needs to be told with clarity, honesty, and a little bit of heart, so that everyone—from the boardroom to the server room—can understand the dragons that lurk just beyond the firewall and the plan to keep them at bay.

But how do you write a story this important? It starts by understanding the essential chapters that make the tale compelling and, most importantly, true.

Chapter One: Know Your Protagonist

Every great story needs a hero. Who is yours? Is your organization a swashbuckling e-commerce startup, navigating the treacherous seas of online retail? Or is it a wise, old financial institution, the stoic guardian of a kingdom's wealth? Maybe it's a healthcare provider, the compassionate keeper of life's most intimate secrets.

You can't tell their story with a generic script. The very soul of your business dictates the nature of the villains you'll face. The startup's greatest fear might be a pirate raid on its payment systems, while the defense contractor's epic involves fending off nation-state spies trying to steal the blueprints to the castle itself.

Your hero's world—their operational landscape—matters just as much. Do they live in a gleaming city in the clouds, trusting their fortunes to outside services? Are they a global fellowship, with outposts scattered across the map? Each detail adds a twist to the plot, introducing new vulnerabilities and challenges. A report that ignores this unique identity isn't just boring; it's a fantasy. It tells a story about a company that doesn't exist.

Chapter Two: The Treasure in the Tower

At the heart of every adventure is a treasure, a "crown jewel" that the hero is sworn to protect. In your story, that treasure is information. But let's be honest, not all loot is created equal. A dusty scroll of old meeting minutes isn't the same as the secret map to the gold.

Effective storytelling requires you to identify what truly matters. What is the one thing that, if stolen, would bring the kingdom to its knees? Is it the personal stories of your customers (PII), which, if leaked, could unleash chaos and ruin trust forever? Is it the secret spells of your source code, the very magic that gives you an edge over your rivals?

A powerful report doesn't just list these assets. It makes the audience feel the weight of their value. It paints a vivid picture of the consequences—the staggering ransoms, the public shame, the operational heart attack—that would follow their loss. It transforms abstract data into something tangible, something worth fighting for.

Chapter Three: The Purpose of the Quest

Why is your hero on this journey? Is it simply to appease the local authorities and stay out of the regulatory dungeons (compliance)? Or is it a grander quest: to build a truly resilient kingdom that can weather any storm and outlast any siege? This is the moral of your story, the guiding North Star for your entire risk management program.

If the goal is just to check a box, your report will read like a legal disclaimer. But if the goal is to build genuine strength, the narrative changes. It becomes a story of proactive defense, of smart investments, and of a culture built on vigilance.

This chapter is also where you define your hero's courage—their risk appetite. How much danger are they willing to face to win the ultimate prize? A high-growth adventurer might take bold risks that a seasoned king would never dream of. By clearly stating this, you give context to the battles you choose to fight and the treasure you're willing to risk. You align the cybersecurity saga with the larger epic of your business strategy.

Chapter Four: The King and His Council

A hero rarely succeeds alone. They need a council of the wise, a fellowship of the brave, and clear lines of command. Without a well-defined governance structure, your story of cyber risk descends into chaos. Who truly owns this tale? Is it the CISO, the brilliant but isolated wizard? The board of directors, watching from their distant throne? Or a dedicated council where all voices are heard?

Great reporting frameworks are like a royal decree, clarifying who is responsible for what. They ensure the scout's urgent warning from the watchtower reaches the general before the battle begins. The report that goes to your tech teams on the front lines will be filled with granular details about the enemy's movements. The version that reaches the board will be a high-level strategic map, showing the state of the kingdom's defenses and the wisdom of its investments.

This structure creates a shared language, a common script that unites the entire cast of characters. It transforms cyber risk from a niche "IT problem" into a core plot point in the business's epic narrative, ensuring that when a decision is made, everyone understands their role and acts in concert.

Ultimately, evaluating a cyber risk framework is about finding the right way to tell your story. It's about choosing a method that captures your unique character, the priceless nature of your treasures, the nobility of your quest, and the strength of your fellowship. When you get that right, the report ceases to be a chore. It becomes your compass, your map, and your chronicle—a powerful tool that empowers you to lead with confidence through the fog of the digital age.

Explanatory notes

Imagine your organization is a ship—let's call it the Enterprise—sailing on a vast, unpredictable digital ocean. Out in these waters, there are treasures to be found: new markets, streamlined operations, incredible connections. But there are also dangers. Not just storms, but phantom currents that can pull you off course, pirate fleets armed with ransomware, and digital krakens lurking in the deep, ready to drag your data down into the abyss.

Just having cannons and a strong hull—your firewalls and antivirus software—isn't enough. The true art of navigating these treacherous waters lies in what your lookouts see and, more importantly, how they report it back to the bridge. A lookout who spots an enemy sail but waits until dinner to mention it has doomed the ship. A report that's just a panicked shout is useless. And a report on the migration patterns of seagulls, while accurate, is irrelevant when a pirate ship is bearing down on you.

This is the soul of cyber risk reporting. It's the constant, critical conversation happening across the entire vessel.

From the Crow's Nest to the Captain's Quarters

Too often, the people in the crow's nest (your brilliant tech teams) shout down in a language only they understand: "SQL injection vulnerability on the aft-database-port-seven!"

To the captain and the ship's investors (your C-suite and board), this is gibberish. They need a translation. They need the First Mate (your CISO or risk officer) to stride onto the bridge and say, "Captain, the lookout has spotted a weakness in our cargo hold. If pirates exploit it, we could lose our entire shipment of gold—that's five million customer records—and face a $50 million penalty from the Crown for unsafe passage. I recommend we reinforce the hull immediately."

Now that is a report. It transforms a technical glitch into a clear and present business danger. It creates urgency. It demands a decision. This is the goal: to turn data into drama, to translate vulnerabilities into vocabulary that affects the bottom line and the brand's survival.

The Ancient Charts of Navigation

Fortunately, we aren't the first to sail these seas. Legendary captains of industry have left us their charts and star maps—frameworks that provide a common language and a proven path to safer harbors.

The NIST CSF: The People's Almanac. Think of this as the most trusted, dog-eared navigator's guide on the ship. It's not a set of rigid laws, but a collection of wisdom: "Here's how to spot trouble (Identify), how to reinforce your ship (Protect), how to know when you've been boarded (Detect), how to fight back (Respond), and how to rebuild afterward (Recover)." It gives everyone on board, from the deckhands to the captain, a shared language to talk about where they are and where they need to go.

ISO 27001: The Royal Navy's Code. This is for the ship that wants the official seal of seaworthiness. It's a formal, rigorous standard that demands you prove your ship is managed with impeccable discipline. To get certified, you must maintain a detailed log—a "Statement of Applicability"—that shows auditors you've thought of every possible risk and have a specific control in place for it. It brings a level of formality that tells the world your vessel is a fortress.

COBIT: The Art of a Profitable Voyage. This framework is bigger than just avoiding pirates. It's about ensuring the entire voyage—from managing the crew to charting the course—serves the ship's ultimate mission: prosperity. COBIT helps the captain ensure that the engine room (IT) is perfectly aligned with the goals of the journey. It reports on risk, yes, but always in the context of, "How is our management of these waters helping us reach our destination wealthier and stronger?"

FAIR: The Spyglass of the Financier. This is a special kind of magic. While other frameworks might say a risk is "High" or "Medium," FAIR provides a powerful lens that translates that risk into dollars and cents. Instead of "There be dragons," FAIR lets you report, "There is a 10% probability of a dragon attack this quarter, which would likely cost us between $1 million and $5 million in lost treasure." For a board that speaks the language of finance, this is the most powerful tool of all. It turns abstract fears into concrete financial forecasts.

Beyond these grand charts, every trade route has its own rules. Financial vessels have specific reporting mandates, as do the ships carrying sensitive healthcare cargo (HIPAA). These are the local maritime laws you must obey or face steep consequences.

Ultimately, surviving and thriving on the digital ocean is a story of communication. It's a continuous cycle of spotting the danger, assessing the threat, taking action, and then telling the story of that risk in a way that everyone on board understands their part to play. With the right approach and the wisdom of these frameworks, your ship won't just avoid the krakens; it will be prepared to discover new worlds, confident that it can weather any storm the digital sea throws its way.

About Author

Azhar ul Haque Sario is a bestselling author and data scientist with a remarkable record of achievement. This Cambridge alumnus brings a wealth of knowledge to his work, holding an MBA, ACCA (Knowledge Level - FTMS College Malaysia and London College of Accountancy, London), BBA, and several Google certifications, including specializations in Google Data Analytics, Google Digital Marketing & E-commerce, and Google Project Management.

With ten years of business experience, Azhar combines practical expertise with his impressive academic background to craft insightful books. His prolific writing has resulted in an astounding 2810 published titles, earning him the record for the maximum Kindle editions and paperback books published by an individual author in one year, awarded by Asia Books of Records in 2024.

ORCID: https://orcid.org/0009-0004-8629-830X
Azhar.sario@hotmail.co.uk
https://www.linkedin.com/in/azharulhaquesario/

www.ingramcontent.com/pod-product-compliance
Lightning Source LLC
Chambersburg PA
CBHW031346230926
51848CB00002B/411
* 9 7 8 3 3 8 4 6 6 5 7 7 5 *